Welcome

The greatest aircraft of all time? Ask ten aviation enthusiasts to name just one, and you'll probably get ten different answers. That said, all would doubtless agree that the Douglas DC-3, the redoubtable Dakota, would be a strong candidate. It's hard to refute it.

Having made its aerial debut in 1935, a few hundred are still flying today, more than 85 years later. That's breathtaking when you pause to consider the multitude of justly famous civil and military types that have come and gone in that time. From the year of its introduction, it was clear that the DC-3 had exceptional qualities – and it was pioneering numerous air travel routes even before World War Two. The conflict that followed changed the world, but the Douglas aircraft arguably enjoyed its finest hour. Military variants not only served as transports but dropped parachutists on D-Day and during Operation Market Garden, alongside many other important assignments, too many to list.

While outclassed as an airliner after the war when technology was leaning towards jet power, the DC-3 lived on, fulfilling a variety of roles with companies all over the world. Relatively simple to operate, robust and reliable, and fantastically versatile, the venerable 'Dak' was the natural solution to many commercial aviation needs. In more recent years survivors have frequently been re-configured to fly passengers again (usually on scenic pleasure flights) or returned to their military livery as airborne memorials.

This reissued special publication offers not just original articles, but also fresh content and previous features from sister publication FlyPast. This includes a wider appreciation of the Dakota's exploits throughout World War Two, personal reminiscences from pilot Jim Tilley, and coverage of existing UK warbirds. Grab yourself a drink, sit back and revel in the stories about this airborne legend.

Chris Clifford
Editor

Chris

BELOW **The unmistakable lines of Douglas' elegant DC-3 are evident in this TWA (Trans World Airlines) machine, NC30079/346**
KEY COLLECTION

Contents

ABOVE The Yorkshire Air Museum's Douglas Dakota Mk.IV G-AMYJ during a fiery nocturnal engine run at its Elvington home on March 14, 2014. See Blighty's 'Daks' on pages 96-97 KEY-JAMIE EWAN

FRONT COVER The Battle of Britain Memorial Flight's Dakota Mk.III performing a crowd-pleasing display at Old Warden, Bedfordshire, in May 2013 DARREN HARBAR

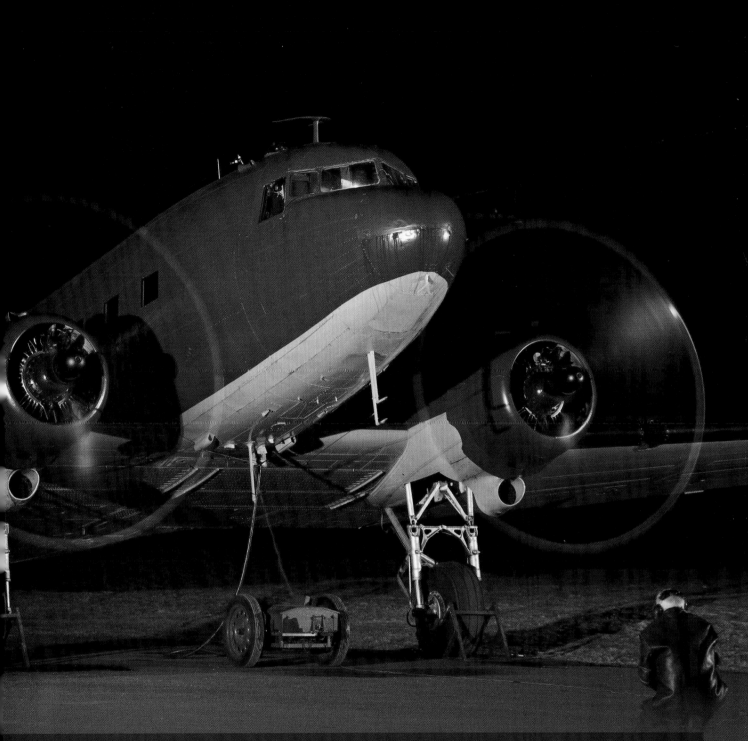

ISBN: 978 1 83632 005 0
Editor: Chris Clifford
Updates, this edition: Mike Haskew
Senior editor, specials: Roger Mortimer
Email: roger.mortimer@keypublishing.com
Cover design: Steve Donovan
Design: Mike Carr and
SJmagic DESIGN SERVICES, India
Advertising sales manager: Sam Clarke
Email: sam.clarke@keypublishing.com
Tel: 01780 755131
Advertising production: Becky Antoniades
Email: Rebecca.antoniades@keypublishing.com

SUBSCRIPTION/MAIL ORDER
Key Publishing Ltd, PO Box 300, Stamford, Lincs,
PE9 1NA
Tel: 01780 480404
Subscriptions email: subs@keypublishing.com

Mail Order email: orders@keypublishing.com
Website: www.keypublishing.com/shop

PUBLISHING
Group CEO and Publisher: Adrian Cox

Published by
Key Publishing Ltd, PO Box 100, Stamford, Lincs,
PE9 1XQ
Tel: 01780 755131 **Website:** www.keypublishing.com

PRINTING
Precision Colour Printing Ltd, Haldane,
Halesfield 1, Telford, Shropshire. TF7 4QQ

DISTRIBUTION
Seymour Distribution Ltd, 2 Poultry Avenue,
London, EC1A 9PU
Enquiries Line: 02074 294000.

A Star
IS BORN

Few aircraft types have had such a lasting impact on the progress of aviation as the iconic Douglas DC-3 and C-47 family. **Malcolm V Lowe** delves into the story of this world famous civil and military transport

BELOW RIGHT Where it all began. The very first Douglas Commercial was the sole DC-1 NC223Y. It proudly wore TWA colours and proved the DC concept, which was refined firstly as the DC-2 and then as the DC-3/C-47 family MALCOLM V LOWE COLLECTION

December 17, 1935 was to become a significant marker in the history of flying machines. Taking to the air that day was the first of what became an extraordinary line of twin-engined transport aircraft in many versions, which collectively have left an indelible imprint on aviation worldwide during the past 85 years. Officially called the Douglas Sleeper Transport (DST), this first example established the basic shape and layout for the thousands of airframes to follow, in a wide variety of different versions for many diverse civil and military roles.

Advanced designs

The Douglas Commercial (DC) series of outstandingly successful airliners began due to a pressing requirement. In the early 1930s, flying the mail was one of the few ways for airlines to stay in business, but as the economy of the US improved following the economic crisis of 1929, the airline industry began to pick up. Aviation design and technology were advancing rapidly throughout the 1930s, leaving behind antiquated biplanes and ushering in the era of the streamlined, fast and powerful monoplane.

The airlines required better and more modern types to replace the ageing, often dangerous, and generally unprofitable passenger-carrying biplane. The US aviation manufacturers Boeing and Douglas were ready to answer this clarion

call. With the twin-engined Model 247 airliner, Boeing created a clean modern-looking design, with advanced features that included all-metal construction, monoplane layout, an enclosed cockpit and passenger cabin, and a retractable main undercarriage. Boeing was a leader with this type of configuration, having designed and built the single-engined Monomail

transport/mail carrier and YB-9 twin-engined bomber. The first Model 247 flew on February 8, 1933, and it became a principal type with United Airlines (written at the time as United Air Lines – UAL – the successor to Boeing Air Transport).

A major rival of UAL, Transcontinental & Western Air (TWA – later Trans World Airlines)

also wanted to buy the Model 247, but this would not have been possible at least until an order of 60 examples for United had been completed. TWA held talks with Douglas to design and build an aircraft that would allow the airline to compete with the Boeing 247s of its major rival UAL.

ABOVE The DC-2 first served militarily with the USAAC as the C-33 (Model DC-2-145). Something of a hybrid, this mark was a military transport specifically for cargo-carrying and had the vertical tail surfaces of the DC-3. Seen here is 36-72, the third production example MALCOLM V LOWE COLLECTION

ABOVE **An iconic image of a famous aeroplane. A significant customer for the DC-3 was American Airlines, whose influence on the creation of the type was considerable. Here, DC-3-277B NC21795 'Flagship Massachusetts' cruises serenely above a snow-covered landscape** AMERICAN AIRLINES

RIGHT **One of several export customers for the DC-2 was the Swiss airline Swissair. Operational from December 1934, HB-ITI was assembled in Europe by Fokker personnel from Douglas-supplied parts, and was thus a Douglas-Fokker DC-2-115B. It was written off during February 1936** SWISSAIR

Douglas' response was the DC-1. Although in the event just a single DC-1 was produced, with the US civil registration NC223Y, this initial Douglas Commercial was the first of the phenomenal line of successful commercial aircraft Douglas was to produce during the coming decades. The DC-1 first flew on July 1, 1933, with test pilot Carl Cover at the controls. A beautifully streamlined twin-engined monoplane with much more attractive lines than Boeing's Model 247, the aircraft was welcomed with enthusiasm by TWA, in whose colours it flew. Basically a 12-seater (to rival the ten seats of its Boeing competition), the DC-1 was accepted by TWA during late 1933 with a few initial modifications. Suitably impressed, the airline subsequently ordered 20 examples of the developed 14-seat production derivative, designated Douglas DC-2.

The new transport was an immediate success. It was flown not just by TWA, but also American Airlines and various other operators. Among several headline-making achievements, the DC-2 PH-AJU of Dutch airline KLM competed in the October 1934 MacRobertson Air Race between London and Melbourne in Australia. It finished an outstanding second, only bettered by a famous purpose-built specialist racer, the de Havilland DH.88 *Grosvenor House*.

Growth potential

It was clear that the excellent design of the DC-1/DC-2 had considerable merit, but that more could be done with the basic layout. The fuselage sides of these initial Douglas Commercials were essentially flat, meaning the fuselage itself could be widened to give more internal capacity. In response to customer suggestions, principally from American Airlines, Douglas' design team revised the DC-2 fuselage configuration, basically by 'rounding-out' the flat fuselage sides to give a virtually circular cross-section. By this simple stroke of genius, the legendary DC-3 was born.

With its big, visibly circular fuselage and two powerful radial engines, the new type looked purposeful from the first. In a twist to the tale, however, the very first example of this new DC airliner was laid out with an interior design that appeared to possibly deliver the best arrangement for its initial purchaser.

The original DST format that first flew during December 1935 offered sleeping berths for its passengers, with an array of small windows above the established main fuselage window arrangement. Standard sleeper accommodation for long-distance night flights was for up to 16 passengers, but this layout was in theory convertible to carry up to 24 daytime passengers.

The DST entered service in the first half of 1936, Douglas having been encouraged to go ahead with the re-design of the DC-2 layout on the promise of orders from American Airlines. Although the sleeper layout was a success, the potential of the type as a pure passenger airliner was obvious from the start, and significant orders began arriving for Douglas to build this variation. The DC-3 therefore 'took-off' in almost breathtaking fashion, propelling Douglas to being one of the world's most important builders of modern, successful commercial aircraft.

It was American Airlines that had the accolade of inaugurating passenger services during June 1936.

The DC-3 was soon realised to be a reliable, fast transport with

excellent range, and it carried passengers in greater comfort than had been known before; it left the Boeing Model 247 miles behind. Prior to the start of World War Two, it pioneered many new air travel routes, and made those existing much more commercially viable. Significantly, it was able to cross the continental US from New York to Los Angeles in some 18 hours and with just three stops. That represented a massive step forward for the later 1930s, and it totally replaced any lingering survivors from the then-antiquated biplane passenger aircraft era.

A further important but often overlooked fact is that the DC-3 was one of the first airliners that could profitably carry passengers alone, without relying on mail subsidies. In that sense it truly represented the emergence of US airlines from the dark days of the economic depression that had commenced during 1929. The type also received significant

export orders from countries world-wide, such was the interest this increasingly successful and popular airliner was able to create.

In the event, the DC-3 was built in several specific versions at Douglas' Santa Monica plant, largely to suit customer preference, although Douglas continued to refine the basic design with various improvements as the type became more successful. Passenger access on these early models was made using a door in the starboard fuselage near the tail, but this arrangement was eventually changed to the port side.

Significant among the major versions was the DC-3A, which introduced the 1,200hp Pratt & Whitney R-1830 Twin Wasp radial engine to the DC-3 line – a move that proved highly important when the type 'donned uniform' and became a pivotal military transport. Prior to that, the Wright R-1820 Cyclone had

been preferred for the DC line, but the Twin Wasp proved to be an excellent engine type for the DC-3.

Civil DC-3 production ended not long after the US entry into World War Two. It is generally accepted that 607 examples were completed from this initial era of the DC-3 story.

Camouflage colours

Even by that time, the DC-3 had been transformed into a military transport, the role for which it is best remembered today. Indeed, the DC line had already experienced considerable military application prior to this due to the DC-2 having been put into action by the then-US Army Air Corps (USAAC). This service used the DC-2 in a variety of versions, notably the C-33 and C-39 transports. Among the first military versions of the DC-2 was also the

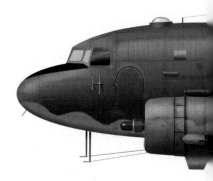

Douglas DC-3A (passenger transport)
Specifications

Powerplant	2 × Pratt & Whitney R-1830-S1C3G Twin Wasp 14-cylinder air-cooled two-row radial piston engines, 1,200hp (895kW) each take-off power
Crew	2-3
Passengers	21-28 (depending on customer preference)
Length	64ft 6in (19.66m) (some sources quote 64ft 8in)
Wingspan	95ft (28.96m)
Empty weight	16,865lb (7,650kg)
Max take-off weight	25,200lb (11,431kg)

Performance

Maximum speed	230mph (370km/h) at 8,500ft
Range	2,125 miles (3,420km)
Service ceiling	23,200ft
Armament	None

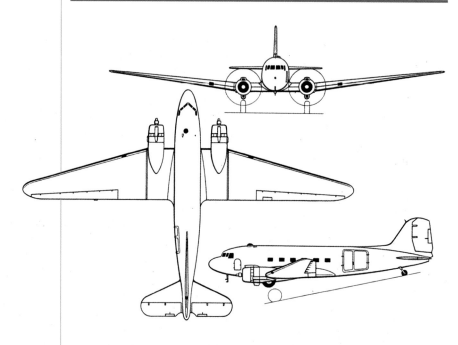

Douglas C-47B Skytrain
Specifications

Powerplant	2 × Pratt & Whitney R-1830-90C Twin Wasp 14-cylinder air-cooled two-row radial piston engines, 1,200hp (895kW) each take-off power
Crew	3-4
Capacity	up to 27-28 troops, or very diverse cargo loads
Length	63ft 9in (19.43m)
Wingspan	95ft 6in (29.11m)
Empty weight	18,135lb (8,226kg)
Max take-off weight	30,000lb (13,608kg)

Performance

Maximum speed	224mph (360km/h) at 10,000ft
Range	1,600 miles (2,575km) (depending on load carried)
Service ceiling	26,400ft
Armament	None

R2D-1 for the US Navy, this type of course being shore based.

At the start of World War Two the DC-3 was the only tried and tested US transport aircraft available in mass production – and therefore potentially available in large numbers. The USAAC embraced the type immediately, and the DC-3 became best known forever after under the US military designation C-47. In fact, there were two main types of military transport based on the DC-3 layout, the C-47 Skytrain and C-53 Skytrooper.

The initial C-47 (Model DC-3A-360) was followed on the Douglas production lines by the C-47A (Model DC-3A-456), which introduced a 24v (in place of a 12v) electrical system, and had numerous changes compared to the civil DC-3. The well-appointed cabin interiors of the civil models were not present in the C-47 line, which naturally had a much more austere internal layout. The floor was strengthened for the carriage of up to some 27 fully equipped troops, paratroopers or around 10,000lb of military cargo including ammunition, parts, general supplies, or even a Jeep. A large cargo door was fitted in the port fuselage side (with its own smaller entrance door), a hoist attachment was available, an astrodome for the cabin roof was introduced, and many examples had a slightly shortened tail cone for a glider-towing attachment. Indeed, towing gliders became an important new role for the C-47 during its service life in World War Two.

The more powerful C-47B (Model DC-3A-467) introduced several improvements, including superchargers for increased altitude 'hot and high' operation.

A new Douglas factory at Long Beach, California was utilised for C-47 production, additional to an operation set up at Oklahoma City (the location was specially built). Alongside the basic troop/paratroop/glider-towing configurations were many different specialist examples, including photographic survey, training, VIP transport and weather recce, to name but a few. Some aircraft acted in the casualty evacuation role or for carrying medical supplies. The type was truly versatile.

The specialized C-53 Skytrooper, which was intended primarily as a troop transport for up to 28 fully equipped soldiers, began production during the second half of 1941 at Douglas' Santa Monica plant. Visibly it lacked the cargo door and hoist attachment of the C-47. Around 400 examples were produced, the far more numerous C-47 line being more versatile and useful.

The US Navy also operated the C-47 in significant numbers. These machines were of course shore based, the C-47 derivatives being designated R4D under the rather ponderous naval classification system. However, they received the C-47 moniker during 1962 when all US military aviation type designations were standardised. The US Navy employed its R4D in various sub-types for training, liaison, VIP transport and an assortment of related second-line duties, including use in Antarctica. The Naval Air Transport Service, founded in late 1941, made good use of it too.

Military production

The C-41 was the first DC-3 derivative to be ordered by the USAAC, although it was something of a hybrid with the DC-2 and was a specialised command transport. The C-41A was a single VIP aircraft supplied to the USAAC during 1939.

The USAAC was transformed into the US Army Air Force(s) (USAAF) during the summer of 1941, and the C-47 immediately became the new command's primary transport. The initial examples of the basic C-47 model were ordered under 1941 Fiscal Year funding, the very first aircraft being serial number 41-7722. It was part of an initial order that included up to 545 examples –a colossal number for its time compared to meagre pre-war contracts. Eventually, according to Douglas' published figures, 965 C-47s were contracted, with 5,254

LEFT **C-47A 42-93098** was specially equipped as a Pathfinder for Ninth Air Force operations and was the first C-47 over Normandy at the start of the D-Day operations, transporting pathfinder paratroopers of the 101st Airborne Division to Sainte-Mère-Église during the night of June 5-6, 1944 KEY-PETE WEST

LEFT **Officially** released in December 1944 although probably taken before then, this photograph demonstrates that a Dakota could accommodate a Jeep internally. However, getting the vehicle in and out of the fuselage was challenging KEY COLLECTION

BELOW **The official** caption states that the personnel in this June 1944 photograph were from the US 101st Airborne Division on the eve of D-Day, but most are actually C-47 aircrew from the unit whose mounts are in the background. The nearest 'CU'-coded C-47A belonged to the 72nd Troop Carrier Squadron of the 434th Troop Carrier Group, Ninth Air Force, at RAF Aldermaston MALCOLM V LOWE COLLECTION

C-47A serial numbers allocated and 3,364 C-47B manufactured. There was even a one-off glider conversion with engines removed and designated XCG-17. In addition, some civil DC-2s and DC-3s were 'impressed' into military service during the war. The DC-3/DST impressments were designated C-48 to C-52, C-68 and C-84.

From the start, the C-47 was hugely successful in military colours. Nevertheless, it was comparatively slow to enter service due to the creation of the new Douglas production lines. Eventually, the C-47 operated in every theatre of war where the US military was in action. By 1944, Skytrains were well established in USAAF service worldwide, and had proved their worth throughout campaigns in the Far East, Pacific, North Africa and the Mediterranean.

One of the first major actions for USAAF C-47s was the Operation Torch landings in North Africa during November 1942. It was to be in northern Europe, however, that the type really gained its thoroughly deserved reputation. Without doubt, it can reasonably be said that the D-Day invasion of occupied France in June 1944 could not have succeeded without the C-47. The type was the first in action at the sharp end, dropping paratroopers and delivering gliders containing airborne soldiers and supplies in the early hours of the invasion. It was truly a vital component of the massive Allied operations at that momentous time.

Other campaigns such the Arnhem landings in September 1944, support for beleaguered Allied forces during the so-called Battle of the Bulge during late 1944, and the Rhine Crossing (Operation Varsity) of March 1945 all featured a significant contribution by the C-47.

Post-war reality

The usefulness of the Skytrain did not cease with the end of World War Two. Indeed, production of the original civil DC-3 was restarted as the DC-3D, using parts left over from wartime contracts when production was run down due to the end of the hostilities.

Two further major military versions of the DC-3/C-47 line were constructed following war's end, the Super DC-3 and C-117.

The former product was launched in the late 1940s as a larger, and more powerful DC-3. It had a lengthened fuselage, squared-off wingtips, revised vertical tail surfaces and more powerful radial engines, either Wright R-1820 Cyclones or the Pratt & Whitney R-2000. However, by then the civilian market was flooded with secondhand military C-47s, which were sold following the end of the war. Many of these were converted to passenger and/or cargo configuration. Ultimately, just five Super DC-3s were completed, with at least three being delivered for commercial use. The prototype Super DC-3 (actually a rebuilt early C-47 designated YC-129) served with the US Navy alongside a number of existing R4Ds upgraded to Super DC-3 specification, under the R4D-8 designation (re-numbered as C-117D during 1962).

The C-117 was a revised C-47B derivative with a modified interior featuring more comfortable seating for 24 passengers, primarily as a staff transport. The main production version was the C-117A, of which only 16 were completed; the ending of World War Two resulted in manufacture being severely curtailed not just of this model, but the whole C-47 manufacturing programme.

Among the many exploits of the DC-3/C-47 during the Cold War era was the Berlin Airlift of 1948-49, in which the type played a significant role flying supplies into the western part of Berlin, which was being blockaded by the Soviet Union and its allies. The C-47 transport aircraft involved were eventually largely replaced in this duty by the bigger Douglas C-54 Skymaster, itself a military version of the civil DC-4 airliner.

However, the C-47 was to play a much more warlike role in the Vietnam War during the 1960s. In this conflict the type flew as a transport for the US forces involved, as well as for the CIA's clandestine airline Air America – but also fought as a gunship for the USAF and eventually the South Vietnamese armed forces. The AC-47 'Spooky' proved deadly in this frontline role, as described on pages 30-37.

Many exports

The DC-3 and C-47 family is one of the most widely exported aircraft types in history. It is almost easier to list the countries that have *not* used DC-3s or C-47s than to compile the long list of operators other than the US, which have used the type in peace or war, civil or military. Countries both large and small have flown it, either for civil use, or military employment… or in many cases both. See pages 38-39 for a map showing the world-wide distribution of DC-3/C-47 operators, by country.

One of the most prolific users of the DC-3/C-47 series was the UK. In British service the type received the name Dakota, and that moniker is often used to describe (somewhat erroneously) the whole family of different types in some publications. Just fewer than 50 RAF squadrons have been identified as having flown 'Daks' at one time or another. The initial use for the RAF was militarised examples of the DC-2, some of which were impressed examples from US airlines. But the main employment involved the C-47-based Dakota, in several specific marks ranging from the Dakota Mk.I to the Mk.IV – the latter being based on the best of the breed, the C-47B. This included considerable use during World War Two, but also for many years after. The type's practicality was underlined by several continuing in support roles for various trials programmes, long after the type had been withdrawn from normal duties. In theory the type is still 'operational' in Britain, due to a single example flown by the Battle of Britain Memorial Flight at RAF Coningsby, Lincolnshire.

Overseas manufacture

Two countries, the Soviet Union and Japan, manufactured the DC-3/C-47 layout in addition to flying examples supplied from Douglas.

A DC-3/C-47 look-alike was the Soviet Union's PS-84/Lisunov Li-2. The Soviet Union made an initial order for a batch of DC-3 transports for the state airline Aeroflot, with 21 examples apparently being delivered up to 1939; two of these airframes are believed to have acted as pattern aircraft for the eventual Soviet licence-production of the DC-3, although some unassembled kits were allegedly supplied to the Soviet Union by Douglas to kick-start Soviet production lines.

The PS-84/Li-2 was markedly different to the C-47, although its cowlings housing the indigenous Shvetsov M-62 (later designated Ash-62) radial engine resembled the early DC-3 examples with their Wright Cyclone engines, in nacelles different compared to, for example, the Pratt & Whitney R-1830 Twin Wasp-powered C-47. Some Soviet machines were armed with a dorsal mid-upper turret, and flexible machine guns could be fired out of cabin windows. The type was also configured as a bomber, whereas USAAF C-47s were never converted for this role and usually flew unarmed. A detailed history of the PS-84/Li-2 is on pages 46-51.

LEFT The C-47 was still a significant cargo aircraft for the USAF years after the end of World War Two. This iconic image shows several Military Air Transport Service C-47s parked at Berlin's Tempelhof airfield during the Berlin Airlift of 1948-49 MALCOLM V LOWE COLLECTION

BELOW C-47A, 43-15501/U5-E, of the 81st Troop Carrier Squadron, 436th Troop Carrier Group, Ninth Air Force, based at RAF Membury, Berkshire, during the D-Day period KEY-PETE WEST

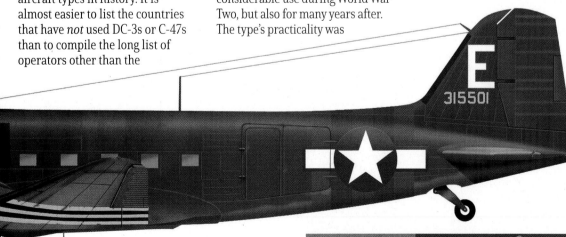

Following World War Two, a number of surviving DC-3 airframes purchased pre-war direct from Douglas for operation by Aeroflot were re-engined with Soviet-produced radial engines, due to there being spares shortages for the Wright Cyclone engines originally supplied with these aircraft.

In Japan, the Shōwa L2D and Nakajima L2D were licence-built derivatives of the DC-3 primarily for military use as the Navy Type 0 Transport. They received the Allied reporting name 'Tabby' during World War Two. After Japan successfully acquired licence DC-2 production rights in 1935, the Japanese company Nakajima gained permission during early 1938 to licence-build the DC-3. It is believed the agreement was for some $90,000.

In similar fashion to production in the Soviet Union, the L2D was modified by the Japanese to suit local standards, measurements, and manufacturing techniques. Power was provided by two Mitsubishi MK8 Kinsei 43 14-cylinder air-cooled radial engines, of some 1,000hp each for take-off.

The Nakajima prototype first flew in October 1939 and production commenced the following year. The L2D was subsequently involved in much action during World War Two, ironically supporting Japanese forces fighting against the US.

According to US intelligence summaries compiled at the end

of the war, 487 'Tabby' airframes were built.

Increased power

The versatility and growth potential of the original DC-3/C-47 layout was demonstrated when the type was deemed suitable for conversion from radial engine power to turboprop. This considerable uprating of the available power, coupled with enhanced performance, guaranteed the survival of the type as a viable transport – and has led to some turboprop examples continuing in frontline service up to the present day.

Among the initial conversions was work performed for British European Airways (BEA) in the late 1940s, when a Dakota was converted to accept Rolls-Royce

Dart turboprops. An intention for this 'Dart-Dakota' was to gain turboprop experience prior to the introduction of the similarly powered Vickers Viscount four-engined airliner.

Since then there has been a wide variety of conversions, some of which have proven more successful than others.

Among the most unusual conversions were the twin-engined turboprop DC-3 make-overs by Conroy Aircraft of Goleta, California. This company's initial type was the Conroy Turbo Three, of which two airframes were converted. The first example was powered by Rolls-Royce Darts from a damaged Viscount airliner. Characterised by very distinctive engine installations – which were markedly different to the

dates from the late 1980s and early 1990s, and so far over 60 examples have been completed, the exact number being difficult to determine due to the use of some airframes in sensitive local conflicts. This is because, in addition to civil use, mainly for survey work in areas such as Antarctica, there is a military version of the BT-67. Drawing on experience with the AC-47 'Spooky' in the Vietnam War, Basler offers a gunship conversion which has been purchased by several countries and is still currently in use; see pages 40-45. Estimates of the combined number manufactured of all DC-3,

see pages 40-45.

original R-1830 Twin Wasp radial engines – the conversion did not find a market although the type's performance was enhanced compared to the basic DC-3 layout. The second conversion (N156WC) was called the Super Turbo Three because it was based on a Super DC-3 airframe.

Following the Turbo Three/Super Turbo Three was the even more radical, three-engined Conroy Tri Turbo Three, which was powered by three Pratt & Whitney Canada PT6A-45 turboprop engines, of some 1,175shp each. One of these power plants was mounted in the nose of the aircraft. It first flew in this converted configuration during November 1977, and was the original Dart-powered Turbo Three rebuilt to this new engine configuration. Thus equipped, and far more powerful that the original DC-3 that it only partly resembled, the aircraft was used in several Polar expeditions, flying in both the Arctic and Antarctic, for which a ski undercarriage was fitted. A second conversion was started after the initial aircraft was damaged by an on-board fire.

Turbo conversion

In South Africa, the need for an uprated version of the DC-3/C-47 line became apparent during the period of internal and external problems in that part of southern Africa. An answer was the BSAS-converted DC-3/C-47 Turbo Dakota, an indigenous modification programme using of a variety of airframes for the South African Air Force by Braddick Specialised Air

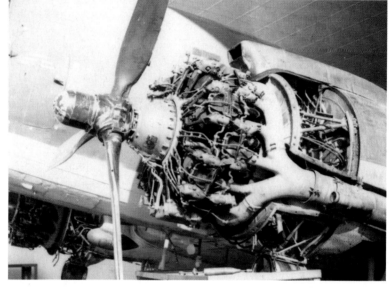

Services International. Powered by two Pratt & Whitney Canada PT6A-65R turboprop engines, the conversion featured revised systems, a stretched fuselage configuration, and modern avionics. Some 50 examples are believed to have been converted to various standards under this programme.

Without doubt, among the most successful and long-lived turboprop conversions of the DC-3/C-47 line is the Basler BT-67. Produced by Basler Turbo Conversions of Oshkosh, Wisconsin, it is a remanufactured and extensively modified DC-3 derivative. The Basler conversion work has included the installation new Pratt & Whitney Canada PT6A-67R turboprop engines, lengthening the fuselage, strengthening the airframe, fitting modern avionics, and various modifications to the wings. The initial conversion work

DST, C-41, C-47, C-53, Li-2, 'Tabby' and the many related versions vary almost as much as the widely published possible production totals. Figures of over 16,000 for all types are often nowadays quoted, but any definite total has to be greeted with a pinch of salt. Writing in the 1980s, DC-3 historian Mike Gradidge quoted a figure of 10,665 DC-3, C-47/C-53/C-117 and US Navy R4D, to which can be added the 487 'Tabby' (L2D) from Japan and the approximately 4,500 plus PS-84/Lisunov Li-2 in the Soviet Union.

Douglas' expansive plant at Santa Monica built the C-41 and C-53 Skytrooper, while the Long Beach and Oklahoma City facilities were responsible for the C-47 line, with the latter also manufacturing the post-war C-117. Santa Monica made all the initial civil DC-3 models, while Oklahoma City built the post-war DC-3D. ●

LEFT **The Conroy Super Turbo Three was one of several attempts to re-engine the DC-3/C-47 with turboprop engines. Seen at Santa Barbara Airport in California, N156WC was based on a Super DC-3 airframe** CHARLES M DANIELS COLLECTION

LEFT **Now situated in modern-day Pakistan, the former RAF Lahore was the location for this RAF Dakota to have its Pratt & Whitney R-1830 Twin Wasp radial engine inspected. The photograph's caption states that 307 MU was based at the airfield** KEY COLLECTION

WORLD WAR TWO
DEFINING DAYS OF THE 'DAK'

When the Dakota first appeared in the skies of Europe during World War Two, it was already a well-established aircraft. But as **Mike Haskew** outlines, the years of conflict are what led to the type becoming a global phenomenon.

The drone of the twin Wasp engines, the anticipation of the mission at hand, and then the sheer number of aircraft that seemed to darken the sky became hallmarks of the military version of the venerable DC-3, the C-47 Skytrain and C-53 Skytrooper to the Americans and the Dakota to the British. And the crucible of World War Two was the transport type's proving ground.

Though the C-47/Dakota flew unarmed, its airlift capability contributed as much or more to the Allied victory in World War Two as any aircraft that took wing during the epic conflict. In all theatres, the beloved militarised DC-3 served, and in doing so the type literally became a war winner. In fact, in his post-World War Two memoir *Crusade in Europe*, General Dwight D. Eisenhower, Supreme Commander Allied Expeditionary Force, credited the C-47 along with the bulldozer and the two and one-half ton truck (the legendary 'deuce and a half') as critical in the defeat of the Nazis in Europe.

Though flown first in 1935 and proposed as a proficient peacetime passenger plane, when war came

the DC-3's conversion proved itself made for the moment. More than 10,000 examples of the C-47 were produced during the war years, and variants of these were flown by each of the major Allied powers. A single C-47 was capable of carrying 18 fully equipped paratroopers or a cargo payload of up to three tons. The heaviest weapon it could transport was the 75mm pack howitzer, which became the standard artillery field gun of the US airborne divisions.

RIGHT **After Operation Overlord, the Allied invasion of Normandy, casualties are loaded aboard a C-47 for transport to medical facilities in England** CREATIVE COMMONS SNORMANDIE VIA WIKIMEDIA COMMONS

RIGHT **Glidermen of the Oxfordshire and Buckinghamshire Light Infantry took Pegasus Bridge in the opening moments of the D-Day invasion** COLLECTIONS OF THE IMPERIAL WAR MUSEUMS VIA WIKIMEDIA COMMONS

RIGHT **Standing beside a C-47 transport, American paratroopers adorn their faces with war paint prior to boarding for the D-Day assault** NATIONAL ARCHIVES AND RECORDS ADMINISTRATION VIA WIKIMEDIA COMMONS

The C-47 could absorb tremendous punishment and remain aloft – many planes returning to base full of holes from enemy shells and shrapnel testifying to its toughness.

Versatile Dakota

The C-47's crew of four - pilot, co-pilot, radio operator, and navigator, praised the plane for its versatility, the ease with which it flew, and its survivability.

The C-47 required only 3,000ft of runway for take-off, and while its average cruising speed was a lumbering 150mph, its range was an impressive 1,500 miles with a service ceiling of 26,400ft. The aircraft could slow to 110mph when the green 'jump' light was illuminated, providing a stable platform for the insertion of airborne troops. Its fuselage door was seven feet wide, allowing easy exit for an airborne soldier burdened with 100lb of combat kit.

At peak production in mid-1943, Douglas was producing more than 100 C-47s per month along with its follow-on C-53 that was configured only to deliver airborne combat troops, not to carry other cargo. While the US Army used the iconic Douglas design widely from the earliest days, RAF Transport Command relied on various modified bomber types to sustain airborne operations before transitioning to the Dakota as the war progressed.

By the spring of 1944, the spectacle of the Allied air transport armada in flight was simply awe inspiring. The C-47 met the challenge of multiple roles, including airborne parachute insertion, glider towing, supply transport, evacuation of wounded, and more.

During the D-Day invasion of Normandy, the Allied airborne vanguard climbed into the night sky, the American 82nd and 101st Airborne Divisions aboard more than 800 transport planes that would drop them behind German lines to secure key roads, bridges, and causeways just inland from the beaches. The Dakotas towed the British 6th Airborne Division, elements of which executed two of the war's most dazzling missions of June 6, 1944, the glider-borne seizure of Pegasus Bridge and the reduction of the Merville Battery.

In the ill-fated Operation Market Garden, Field Marshal Bernard Montgomery's combined airborne/ground offensive aimed at the capture of vital bridges across waterways of the southern Netherlands with a dagger thrust into the Ruhr, the British RAF Transport Command and the US IX Troop Carrier Command put 1,438 C-47/Dakota transports in the air, delivering three airborne divisions, the US 82nd and 101st and the British 1st, across more than 60 miles in a broad daylight airdrop and glider insertion. In the September 1944 operation, they towed more than 2,100 Airspeed Horsa, General Aircraft Hamilcar, and CG 4 Waco gliders.

All the while, the dependable Douglas design was in short supply, and the lack of available transport planes resulted in a need for multiple missions to deliver men and equipment to the Market Garden zone of operations. In typical fashion, the C-47 pilots and aircrew braved anti-aircraft fire, occasional German fighter intervention, and their own fatigue and exhaustion from continuing sorties in support of the offensive.

Operation Torch

The C-47 really earned its combat spurs during the North Africa campaign in 1942 as Allied troops came ashore at Casablanca, Oran,

ABOVE LEFT **An American C-47 Skytrain flies over the pyramids of Egypt in 1944. The C-47 was the workhorse of Allied air transport** US AIR FORCE VIA WIKIMEDIA COMMONS

ABOVE RIGHT **C-47s and Waco gliders sit ready to depart an English airfield during Operation Varsity, the airborne crossing of the River Rhine, in March 1945** US AIR FORCE VIA WIKIMEDIA COMMONS

BELOW **Dozens of C-47 Skytrain transport planes release their cargoes of 82nd Airborne Division paratroopers during Operation Market Garden** US ARMY VIA WIKIMEDIA COMMONS

ABOVE **Parachutes billow as US airborne troops pour from the open doors of C-47 transports during Operation Market Garden** US ARMY VIA WIKIMEDIA COMMONS

RIGHT **Paras of the British 1st Airborne Division smile after clambering aboard a Dakota transport prior to parachuting into the Netherlands during Operation Market Garden** COLLECTIONS OF THE IMPERIAL WAR MUSEUMS VIA WIKIMEDIA COMMONS

RIGHT **Surrounded at Bastogne, troopers of the US 101st Airborne Division watch as C-47s parachute badly needed supplies during a critical stage of the Battle of the Bulge** US ARMY SIGNAL CORPS VIA WIKIMEDIA COMMONS

time operations, had to be located as far from prying German eyes as possible to maintain secrecy while fuel capacity dictated that they should be as close as possible to keep the mission within range of the African continent. Survey crews scoured the countryside around Land's End at the southwestern tip of England and settled on two small airfields at St. Eval and Predannack. The flight path, a straight-line distance of 1,100 miles, would cross the airspace of neutral Spain. Although the right-wing Spanish government of Generalissimo Francisco Franco was sympathetic to the Nazis and Spanish Air Force fighters might intervene, such risk was deemed acceptable.

Worthy of note is the fact that a mere 39 C-47s were allotted to the Torch airborne insertion with 531 paratroopers aboard. Such numbers were obviously dwarfed later in the war with the exponential growth of airborne forces.

Even as Operation Torch proceeded, Operation Husky, the invasion of Sicily undertaken on July 9, 1943, was being planned. Both Montgomery and American General George S. Patton, Jr., considered an airborne prelude to the landings of their Eighth and Seventh Armies, respectively, essential to the success of the first major Allied offensive against Axis home territory. The airborne aspect

and Algiers during Operation Torch that November. Plans for airborne troops to participate in the operations at Casablanca and Algiers were considered and then shelved, but concerns surrounding a pair of Vichy French airfields near Gibraltar, just a hop across the narrows of the Mediterranean and a threat to the Allied landings, prompted the deployment of the US 2nd Battalion, 509th Parachute Infantry Regiment, which then made the first combat jump in American military history.

That first American airborne combat operation remains the longest of its kind in the history of airborne warfare. The situation presented something of a conundrum as the C-47s, for all practical purposes untried in real-

of Operation Husky, launched from airfields in North Africa, produced a mixed bag of triumph and tragedy. While the paratroopers made their presence known in tough combat with the Germans, their drops were scattered across a wide area, which led to small groups battling the enemy as best they could.

The British glider force, a substantial element of 2,075 men, was the vanguard of the entire operation, and 109 Dakotas in concert with 35 Armstrong Whitworth Albemarle transports towed 144 Waco and Horsa gliders loaded with troops into difficult weather conditions that contributed greatly to what may be deemed a debacle. High winds buffeted the Dakotas and Albemarles, six of which never got out of North African airspace. Some transport pilots became lost and turned back with their gliders still in tow. A few towlines snapped, the gliders plummeting into the sea. Some transports simply disappeared, and an estimated 70 gliders were either released too soon or in the wrong area. Troop Carrier Command concluded that only 58 gliders landed in Sicily at all while 605 glidermen were lost, 326 missing and presumed drowned.

Friendly Fire

Meanwhile, a reinforcing airborne flight was scheduled for the night of July 11, and one of the worst friendly fire incidents of World War Two occurred. Although some precautions had been taken to alert anti-aircraft batteries ashore and ships off the Sicilian coast, the 144 C-47s of the US 313th and 61st Troop Carrier Groups were subjected to a torrent of fire from jittery crews that had experienced numerous enemy air raids during the previous 24 hours.

Captain Adam A. Komasa of the 504th Parachute Infantry Regiment recalled: "It was an uncomfortable feeling knowing that our own troops were throwing everything they had at us. Planes dropped out of formation and crashed into the sea. Others, like clumsy whales, wheeled and attempted to get beyond the flak which rose

in fountains of fire, lighting the stricken faces of men as they stared through the windows."

When the ordeal was finally over, 23 precious C-47s had been shot down and another 37 damaged. Casualties topped 400 airborne and troop carrier personnel. Ground crewmen counted 1,000 bullet holes in the wings and fuselage of one Skytrain that managed to return to base.

Despite such a dismal day, the rugged C-47/Dakotas and the crews that manned them persevered through operations in Italy and southern France. During the pivotal Battle of the Bulge, the C-47s supplied the beleaguered defenders of the crossroads town of Bastogne by air amid flying conditions that were often less than ideal. On the other side of the world, the Skytrain was an early participant in the war against Imperial Japan. The C-47 performed supply and airborne missions in the China-Burma-India theatre, New Guinea, the Philippines, and elsewhere.

With the Third Reich in its death throes in the spring of 1945, the C-47/Dakota was the primary airlift tool that executed Operation Varsity, the airborne crossing of the great River Rhine in concert with Montgomery's Operation Plunder, the Allied ground offensive across the natural barrier and the German frontier. Operation Varsity was a tremendous undertaking. In the event, the airborne armada stretched from horizon to horizon as 21,680 paratroopers and glidermen of the First Allied

Airborne Army flew into battle aboard 1,696 transports and 1,348 gliders.

When the greatest armed conflict in human history finally ended in 1945, the battle-tested Douglas DC-3 – in its combat role as the C-47/Dakota – had contributed mightily to the hard-won Allied victory. Other conflicts would emerge in later years, and the proven transport would again respond to the call. But there is no doubt that the epic trial of World War Two defined the C-47/Dakota's place in history, etching its finest hour of performance in the process. ●

Just a 'SPROG' pilot

Having Befriended former RAF pilot Jim Tilley, Steve Richards shares some of the Airman's memories of flying Dakotas immediately after World War Two

I got to know Jim Tilley quite well during the late 1990s, shortly before he died. I always remember asking him if he recalled any particularly 'hairy' moments, to which he replied in a somewhat serious tone: "I nearly lost one of my crew out of the back door. We often practised dropping heavy supply containers, which we did from slightly lower than 200ft. No parachutes or anything, just freefall. For this role, the cabin had a conveyer installed to get the cargo out as quick as possible. These containers would 'whoosh' through the fuselage over the steel rollers and were then pushed out the cargo

door. One of the lads got hit in the back of the legs by a load and very nearly went out with it!"

African Excursion

That was on October 22, 1945 when flying as the second pilot in Douglas Dakota Mk.III KG671 from RAF Welford, Berkshire. However, just over 18 months before in early 1944, Jim, aged just 19, arrived at Mount Hampden located 11 miles (17km) from Zimbabwe's capital city Harare, eager to learn how to fly. Posted to the Rhodesian Air Training Group's 28 Elementary Flying Training School (EFTS), the rugged Fairchild Fleet Cornell II basic trainer awaited him.

With his first flight on February 2, 1944, Tilley went solo just eight days later before gaining his wings in mid-April. Deemed above average as both a pilot and navigator, he was posted to 23 Service Flying Training School at RAF Heany, about 220 miles (354km) southwest, for multi-engine training later that month. Equipped with Airspeed Oxford Mk.Is and several Avro Anson Mk.Is, Jim soloed within six days having mastered an aeroplane with two engines and a retractable undercarriage. Building his hours and experience on both types, by October his logbook recorded more than 200 flying hours. Considered

competent, the young pilot was sent to RAF Qastina, Palestine in mid-January 1945 to join 77 Operational Training Unit equipped with Vickers-Armstrong Wellington B.Xs. Graded as proficient in early March, Tilley expected to return to Europe and join an operational squadron. At the time though, the war in Europe was rapidly concluding and the need for transport crews had become far more pressing. However, as is the nature of war, progressive events in the field often made it essential to frequently change the rules and regulations – leading to delays in knowing where he was required. With no operational posting coming his way, Fg Off Tilley, as he was

now, found himself back in the UK marking time as a fully qualified pilot with nothing to fly. He joined 11 EFTS at Perth Airfield, Scotland, as an instructor on the de Havilland Tiger Moth, which allowed him to keep flying but, more importantly, collect his flight pay while doing so.

Dakota Driver

Eventually, in late September 1945, Jim joined 1336 Transport Support Conversion Unit at RAF Welford with the Douglas Dakota. He recalled: "There was a need for crews to provide tactical support glider towing, as well as dropping parachutists and supplies. I remember the Dakota having

ABOVE **A flight of six RAF Dakotas. More than 1,900 of the type were supplied to the RAF, under the USA Lend-Lease programme during World War Two, and flown by some 46 squadrons, plus support units** ALL KEY COLLECTION UNLESS STATED

BELOW **Fairchild's Fleet Cornell was used extensively throughout the Commonwealth Air Training Scheme for basic pilot training. Jim Tilley first flew the type on February 2, 1944** VIA DAVID NEWNHAM

ABOVE **A war-weary RAF Dakota, moments from touching down after another supply drop. Jim recalled the type having decent brakes.**

decent brakes. The Wellington had very inefficient brakes and when taxiing it, I was always petrified of pranging the thing into other aircraft. On the Dakota, the brakes were, I think, hydraulic and they worked a treat." Following his first flight in the Douglas machine, it took just 13 further trips totalling 19 hours to complete his conversion. Among the Dakotas that Jim was introduced to were KG321 and KG452, both Mk.IIIs. Jim smiled and chuckled as he recalled: "Up until the Dakota, I had always flown with a parachute either clipped to my chest or, more often, sat uncomfortably on one. But now because I was in a transport aircraft, they weren't deemed necessary and we sat on very comfy seats.

"Between the two pilot seats was a Radio Direction Finder [RDF] with a tuning dial. Flying at night [his logbooks show this was often in Dakota Mk.III KG650] around Berkshire in autumn 1945, we would tune the RDF into the American Forces Network. There we were, cruising around the sky in

a relatively plush American airliner listening to the American big bands – it was absolutely great."

Settling into life on the squadron, Jim's logbooks note he was taught the art of glider towing at Welford's satellite airfield RAF Ramsbury, 9 miles (15km) to the west. Entries show this normally involved cross-country flights exceeding 90 minutes during the day and just 20 minutes at night. Interspersed throughout are sorties dropping paratroopers over the grass air strip at Netheravon, Wiltshire from Dakota FZ625, and supply drops out of KG650.

Heavy Haulers

An often overlooked role of the Dakota was the retrieval of gliders, known to the crews as 'snatch'. Jim continued: "We practised this at RAF Ramsbury. There they would firmly secure two poles about 15ft high, with a cable draped between them that extended out to a glider, forming a triangle. For this role, the 'Dak' had a hook fitted to the lower fuselage and the idea was to fly across the field at about 20ft with

it trailing, snatch at the cable and scoop up the glider. We would then complete a circuit of the field with it behind us before releasing it." This tactic was used throughout the Far East for medical evacuations where gliders full of wounded personnel would be snatched from fields unsuitable for landing Dakotas.

Jim laughed as he continued: "There were lots of amusing stories though, including one where the pilot lowered the hook, came down low too early and then arrived at the practice field with an apple tree and two hawthorn bushes in tow."

> ## "The Wellington had very inefficient brakes and when taxiing it, I was always petrified of pranging the thing into other aircraft"

This technique was effective but also incredibly hazardous. Within six to seven seconds the waiting glider would go from stationary to more than 100mph (160km/h) once caught. But as the slack disappeared, the glider's nose would drop while the tail rose dramatically before rapidly leaping into the air. The strain on both glider and Dakota was huge, as Jim remembered: "We always had to watch the speed fall off as we made the snatch."

For training purposes, gliders were fitted with concrete blocks as ballast to represent their operational weights – normally about a third of the tow aircraft. The long hook beneath the Dakota was fitted to a torsion bar, which was essentially a spring not unlike the mainspring in a clockwork device, to help absorb the shock. But as Jim noted: "I was always glad to be in the 'Dak' and not in the glider."

With his type training completed towards the end of 1945, the RAF soon had Jim heading for Singapore to join a VIP transport squadron with Air Command's South East Asia Communications Squadron.

BELOW **A Douglas Dakota tug runs in to 'snatch' a Waco GC-4 Hadrian II glider circa 1945. Although the technique was effective, it was also incredibly hazardous.**

Departing from southern England in an Avro York, he spent Christmas in Pakistan's capital Karachi. Jim grimaced as he jokingly said: "…my stomach has only just recovered."

Rookie Ride

Eventually arriving in the Far East, Jim undertook his first flight from RAF Changi, Singapore with his new unit on March 5, 1946. He explained: "The squadron's principal purpose was to look after and fly the personal aircraft allocated to the South East Asia theatre British Commanders-in-Chief – Arthur Tedder of the air force, Miles Dempsey of the army and, of course, Lord Louis Mountbatten. The latter's Dakota was named *Sister Ann*, but he also had a York and a second Dakota named *Mercury*. That aircraft was crammed with special state-of-the-art airborne wireless and cipher kit. *Mercury* could transmit and receive signals from London while flying over Delhi – no mean feat in 1946.

"Of course, I was only a 'sprog' pilot, while the others on the squadron were real old sweats with thousands of flying hours in their logbooks. I did fly as co-pilot for Dempsey on half a dozen occasions in his aircraft. He called it *Lilli Marlene*."

Jim and his crewmates were kept busy, usually flying lower-ranked VIPs all over Southeast Asia. One flight from Batavia (now Jakarta) to Changi, in Dakota KG761, stands out in particular for Jim: "We'd flown some passengers down to Java and for the return trip to Singapore we were given two passengers – a wing commander and a squadron leader.

You must keep in mind, I was only a lowly flying officer at this stage. About halfway back, we flew into some filthy weather – thick black stuff that you don't see in Europe. We tried to go over it, but it was too high. We tried to go under it, but it was too close to the sea for us. So, we just went through it at about 2,000ft and, unexpectedly, it wasn't excessively bumpy. When the two passengers got out, they said to me 'well done. We always thought it could be done.' Afterwards, I said to my co-pilot, 'What was all that about?', he just shrugged. Later in the mess, our flight was the talk of the old hands. 'Hear about that flight from Java today, it must have been a 'sprog' crew? They flew through all that muck!' Evidently, the experienced pilots wouldn't go near that type of Far Eastern storm cloud, and the proper course of action would have been to turn back, but as they say, ignorance is bliss."

In mid-1946, Tilley had the chance to fly a type used primarily by the RAF in the Far East, the Beechcraft C-45F Expeditor Mk.II – KJ479 being the machine in question. However, two entries close together in Jim's logbook, dated July 21,

are especially noteworthy. These record two short flights – one of 45 minutes' duration and the other of 35 – from his home base of Changi. Under the 'Duty' column is printed 'SPRAY SINGAPORE' and where the aircraft's serial is normally noted it simply reads 'DDT'. About this time, Far East-based RAF Dakotas were the preferred platform for insecticide spraying duties employing dichlorodiphenyltrichloroethane – more commonly abbreviated to DDT. It has since been banned in some countries after being linked with cancer-causing agents.

Not long after, on July 28, Tilley captained Dakota KG761 from Penang, Malaysia to Changi for his final flight – like Jim, the aircraft was also coming to the end of its RAF career. In 1950, he married his fiancé Lesley and the honeymoon was to be in Jersey. The couple turned up at Birmingham Airport for the flight – ironically it was aboard a British European Airways Dakota.

James Tilley died in July 1999, aged 75 years.

He had flown the Dakota for little over a year, yet had become a 'Dak' master in all weathers. ●

ABOVE LEFT Converting to the 'Dak' in 1945, Jim became proficient in 'snatching' gliders soon after. Here a Dakota snags the towing cable with its specially designed hook.

ABOVE RIGHT A close-up of the hook in action. The cable, which was connected to the glider, would be draped between two 15ft poles to form a triangle. Aircraft performing the 'snatch' would fly as low as 20ft.

BELOW Jim was sent to fly the Vickers Wellington in January 1945 after completing his twin-engined training on the Anson and Oxford.

Damn Near
KILLED US...

Robert S Grant reveals the intricacies and hardships of operating ski-equipped DC-3s during the height of winter in Canada

Like so many aviation collections, the Canada Aviation and Space Museum in Ottawa exhibits a magnificent looking Douglas DC-3. Here, visitors can gaze upon this example of mechanical grace in comfort, and never concern themselves with frozen body parts or frost-crusted eyebrows. However, many pilots, mechanics and passengers cannot forget – or forgive – their association with what Canadians across the sub-zero wilderness knew simply as the 'Three'. In spite of body-numbing low temperatures where grease and sandwiches turned hard amid snow, sleet, and hail, DC-3s performed tasks unlikely imagined when test pilot Carl A Cover flew the prototype through California's congenial skies on December 17, 1935.

Rough ride
Frozen digits became a trademark for flight crews, as not-so-gentle monikers followed the type into 'miles and miles of nowhere'. What British journalist William Stancliffe Shackleton once termed as the "gentleman's boudoir" became the facetiously labelled 'Rectus?

Damnnear Killedus' (Wrecked us? Damn near killed us). Animal trappers, Indians and prospectors forced to endure turbulent air as they flew into bleak glacial terrain preferred the term 'Vomit Comet'.

Across the ice-locked tundra of central Quebec, geologists discovered iron deposits 317 miles north of the Gulf of Saint Lawrence. Penetrating rock mantles and harvesting the ore entailed a massive enterprise, which led to the creation of Hollinger Ungava Transport in 1948. To jump-start the project, Canadian Pacific Airlines (CPA) manager and

ex-bush pilot Walter 'Babe' Woollett borrowed wooden skis for a DC-3 from the USAF, in exchange for performance reports.

Attached to CPA's Olive Drab airframe CF-CPV, the laminated units resembled flying boxes with streamlined plywood fairings. In flight, they required higher than normal engine power, and while taxiing, the lack of cooling airflow regularly forced cylinder head temperatures into the red. Based at Mont-Joli on the St Lawrence River, mechanics ignored polar-like gales and busied themselves with nails and glue, while hooded loaders

struggled to insert Caterpillar tractors destined for remote areas too small to accommodate wheel-equipped machines. "The wooden skis didn't last long and caused about a 20% deterioration in performance compared to metal examples," recalled Capt G H Wurtele in the January 1982 issue of *Air Classics*. He added: "Cruise never exceeded 122kts, but take-off and landing speeds were normal. They weren't retractable so the wheels were removed." While Hollinger Ungava's invasion into the wilderness with wooden ski-equipped DC-3s was a success, by

ABOVE **The crew of Air Dale DC-3 C-FOOW exercise the aircraft's wheel-skis en route to Pickle Lake in the Canadian province of Ontario** ALL IMAGES ROBERT S GRANT UNLESS STATED

BELOW **Air Dale operated Douglas DC-3 C-FOOW,** pictured here on Ontario's Opapimiskan Lake, while delivering construction materials and equipment to a nearby gold mine in January 1983

ABOVE **A close up of a DC-3's wheel-ski arrangement – each pair weighed slightly more than 1,000lb**

ABOVE RIGHT **Given the brutally low temperatures, DC-3 brakes repeatedly froze – forcing engineers to use hot air from electrically fired Herman Nelson heaters to thaw the units. Once finished, the hoses were inserted under the engine quilts to warm the cylinders and oil coolers**

RIGHT **Lightweight bulldozers were often deposited on snow-covered lakes to clear airstrips for wheeled aircraft. In some cases, the machine remained behind to shunt awkward freight**

1946, all-metal wheel-ski examples had arrived. Following evaluation in the midwestern US state of North Dakota and Canada's Alberta, Minneapolis' Federal Aircraft Works produced at least 200 pairs, which soon became standard.

Provincial lifeline

Field Aviation of Calgary revealed that a pair of skis, including axles, bearings, and clamps, weighed 1,053lb. The main 'boards' – as mechanics dubbed them – measured almost 14ft and reduced airspeed by less than 5mph. "They are unique because they appear to be just additional dead weight, but they are, in fact, a very aerodynamically designed tool," commented former Air-Dale Dakota pilot Murray Ferguson, who added: "The leading edge is cambered toward the trailing edge so that resultant air pressure passing by the ski flows smoothly back, thus reducing mainplane stall characteristics at slow speed."

When parked, pilots selected the skis up, to avoid them freezing to the surface. On several occasions, inexperienced ground handlers overlooked the basic physics principal that weight generated heat – and returned to find the skis 'welded' to the ice. At an average weight of 27,000lb, a DC-3 could not be rocked free like some lightweight bush aircraft! As penalties, the crews laboured with shovels, steel bars and wooden

blocks to break them loose. Once they managed that, more backbreaking work awaited, as an empty 905sq ft cargo compartment did not garner revenue.

Snowmobiles, diesel generators and palletised necessities such as odoriferous onion sacks and disposable diapers needed winching, or pushing, up snow-covered floors angled upward at 17°. As many as 16 metal drums weighing 450lb each became routine cargo – each one a deadly missile if the straps securing them snapped. With Dakotas often the only mode of transport, coffins were frequently carried… embalming fluids soaked boots, while plywood splinters pierced palms. Instead of reposing in airport lounges, pilots bent backs,

> **"As many as 16 metal drums weighing 450lb each became routine cargo – each one a deadly missile if the straps securing them snapped"**

scraped scalps, and rushed to escape forbidden night landings or ice fog raging over the ragged territory. Haste occasionally led to the aircraft's weight creeping beyond legal limits.

In one documented incident, the crew pondered their sluggish climb, and a quick check of the manifest confirmed a planned load of 6,000lb. But despatchers later discovered the paperwork was incorrect. The machine had climbed into the winter dawn carrying almost twice that figure. A similar miscalculation led to an unofficial cargo record for Douglas' example of aerial perfection and its multicellular three-section wing – an incredible 14,768lb.

Weary workhorses

However, these DC-3s did not shine like the Finnair-marked OH-LCH serenely sailing to airshows, or Breitling's former HB-IRJ hauling Navitimer watches around the world today. Spluttering forklift trucks frequently left signature punctures in fuselages, while ragged tape revealed where previous collisions had been patched. Maintenance-engineer and pilot Hartley Weston recalled seeing a ski-equipped 'Dak' smashing through sun-softened crust and shattered ice. Unknown to the crew, the fabric had separated from the elevators during their take-off roll. At full power and the column pulled back to its stops, the aircraft staggered into a vertical climb and suddenly plummeted, before vanishing from sight. It then reappeared as the crew fought for their lives and struggled over the lake's coniferous shoreline, slamming tail-first onto a nearby airstrip. Weston rushed to the machine as the pilots wobbled out. Except for the crinkling metals of the overheated engines and sizzles of hot oil on the snow, not a sound rived the silence. He remembered: "All you could see was those guys' eyeballs! They had their flight bags and sleeping bags and walked right past me and never said a word. They got on a bus leaving town – I never saw them again."

Northern-based pilots, nurtured in the white-on-white world beyond their four-piece windscreens, climbed aboard their Threes with complete confidence in themselves and the 'old girls' – despite facing repeated cracked crankcases and blown cylinders. There were no gold stripes or smart uniforms either, just oversized coveralls holed by battery acid and whitened by cement dust. Inside the stressed-skin machines they were dragging across the so called 'slabs of hell', there were no carpets to soften steps. "On entering the cave-like cargo compartment, you could not help but notice C-GNNA's body odour – a fragrance of zinc chromate, fuel and engine oil, hydraulic fluid, alcohol and cigarettes. The floor was tattered half-inch plywood once painted grey – sand sprinkled on it so crews could navigate the steep gradient to the cockpit," recounted Skymark Airlines Boeing 737 captain Samuel

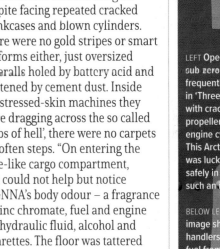

LEFT Operating in sub zero conditions frequently resulted in 'Threes' landing with cracked propeller seals or engine cylinders. This Arctic Air DC-3 was lucky to land safely in 1974 after such an incident

BELOW LEFT This 1980 image shows ground handlers transferring fuel from an Austin Air DC-3's cabin bladder tanks, while at a Cree Indian reserve. It was a habitually messy job

ABOVE **Pack it tight:** Once on the ground DC-3 pilots would taxi around in circles to compress the surface, which made manoeuvring easier. Here, a Dale Air airframe awaits its next load

RIGHT **Although** Douglas DC-3 C-FBXY never operated with wheel-skis, Sabourin Lake Airways flew it year-round. Note the wide, low-pressure tyres, which allowed the aircraft to move on snow-covered surfaces other freighters often could not negotiate

Cole. His 2018 book, *Instruments, Switches, Radios and Rudders,* has become a northern flying classic. Before considering off-strip operations, most air services dispatched a smaller aircraft to scrutinise the thickness of the ice. One pilot recalled that at least 24in was needed to support a DC-3 – although it varied between locations. Pre-flight duties in the dim light of morning proved no walk-in-the-park for mechanics as they repeatedly replaced hoses shattered by the cold and scraped the frozen windshields. Support staff used brooms to spread costly de-icing fluid over the aircraft's 95ft wings, as they inhaled eye-watering fuel fumes. Ignoring runny noses and cold-scorched hands, pilots helped roll out gigantic heaters to warm each of the 1,200hp Pratt & Whitney R-1830's 28 cylinders. Cold-stiffened engine tents were hurled into baggage compartments ready to be used again at the next destination, as unloading

times ate into the powerplants' residual warmth.

When empty, a typical DC-3 with minimal equipment weighed about 17,755lb. While working for Austin Airways, Cole remembered multiple 55-mile flights from northwest Ontario's Red Lake to the Cree settlement of Pikangikum with 8,100lb of cargo and just 1,000lb of fuel.

Gem hunters

In the mid-1990s, Buffalo Airways pilots utilised a 1,750ft airstrip 190 miles northeast of Yellowknife in the Northwest Territories, to help establish Canada's first diamond mine. Working with the

mining company, both contended with short daylight hours and frequent white-outs, where pilots pushed through skies hypnotically blending with the surface.

Before activating buzzing boost pumps and snapping solenoids, aircrew ensured the engine's oil temperature reached at least 50°F after the external heaters had been dragged clear. With a steady bluish-white exhaust indicating all 36 spark plugs were firing, each 446lb three-bladed propeller coiled hurricane-scale storms backwards. Up in the cockpit, pilots hoped for follow-up heat from the powerplants, but despite a myriad of manifolds, valves, and ducts, they rarely enjoyed

complete comfort. Austin Airways' C-GNNA had a pipe protruding into the navigator's compartment that would supposedly warm the entire aircraft; the absence of headliners only exacerbated the chill. "If you mismanaged the engines after start-up, you could split a cooler due to the fact the oil had congealed," recalled Cole, adding: "Of course, cylinders cracked from the shock cooling and over boosting in the cold dense air. Sometimes, a leaky oil cooler slathered the brake discs, so when you applied them, they would heat it up and catch fire."

Tentatively teasing

On the move, aircrew dared not close the throttles too far in fear of becoming caught up by the friction-heated ski bottoms. When the surface was sticky, the engines rarely produced sufficient power to overcome the type's distinctive left swing caused by engine and propeller torque. As such, taking off in a wide left-handed curve became

normal when operating from large lakes. Passengers detested low-level turbulence and many never refined the skill of opening airsickness bags – left over residue often turning putrid when the warm season arrived.

Frequently, contaminated spark plugs accounted for long delays. Following start-up, carburettor heat

helped prevent fouling, until forced prolonged slow idling prompted rough running and unacceptable magneto drops. Austin Airways mandated pushing the powerplants to 1,600rpm for three minutes, with a maximum temperature 446.9°F. Ferguson recommended cautious throttle movements, while the Royal Canadian Air Force warned about over boosting – all too easily done when taxiing across undulating snow drifts.

Before the battle to flog a multi-ton metal box into the sky commenced, pre-departure checks included 1/4 flap down. Jeffrey Schroeder, a veteran Curtiss C-46 and DC-3 pilot with Buffalo Airways, described taking off as "making power" as the more than 11ft Hamilton Standard propellers converted wintry greeting card scenes into arenas of blasting and pushing. With the throttles

forced to a quivering 48in hg (a unit for pressure) and 2,700rpm, observers would lose sight of the aeroplane and its wobbling wings in clouds of watery slush. "During take-off, initial acceleration is very slow and subsequently deceleration is rapid. Directional control is maintained by use of rudder and partial brake when available," explained Ferguson. "The aircraft is flown off the ice in a tail-down attitude at a book speed of 65-75kts, but I've flown off the surface at 50kts. One ponders in disbelief of the Three's capabilities."

When clear, the aircraft was levelled until the speed had crawled past 89mph while the skis remained down until the airspeed indicator showed 109mph. Once selected 'up', the skis sat against protective rubber pads on the engine nacelles. However, in the cockpit the pilots did not relax until raising the flaps and managing the engines to climb at 137mph.

Aiming to cruise at 159mph, the R-1830s would be set at 28in hg for 2,050rpm, which usually consumed around 540lb of fuel per hour.

However, winter DC-3 pilots could never rest completely – especially when it came to maintaining compass headings in the pre-GPS and autopilot eras. Navigational equipment generally consisted of coffee-stained paper maps with dull pencil marks. Although the 8 1/3 imp gal hydraulic tank was filled to the brim, constantly bleeding pressure allowed the wheels to randomly lower themselves. This forced either pilot to pump a gigantic handle

beside the co-pilot's seat to replenish the system – steam emanating from their parkas formed an opaque varnish on the cockpit windscreen as they did.

Torturous luck
Controlling surface contamination became an art form. Alcohol-based defrosting fluids cleared windscreens, but when the piquant odour diminished, the supply reservoir had run out – there was never enough. "The windshield alcohol didn't work," mused Cole. "I would have to open the side window and force my mitten-covered hand out with a scraper to see enough to land." The same liquid was used to protect the props. When loosened, huge chunks of ice slammed against the fuselage, making everyone on board jump. Mechanics waxed the wing boots with furniture polish and in the air, crews waited until ice accrued to around half-an-inch before activating them.

On December 6, 1972 Superior Airways DC-3 CF-AUQ encountered freezing precipitation while heading to a lake near Quebec. The

captain asked his co-pilot to take control while he utilised Cole's technique to clear the windscreen. Resuming command, he discovered the co-pilot had allowed the aircraft to enter a right-hand spiral descent – he barely recovered the machine in time but managed to save the lives of all three on board.

Besides white-out and unexpected descents, slush stood out as the hazard most feared. To the uninitiated, landing areas appeared as sparkling crystal carpets where wild animals frolicked, but realistically, top snow layers insulating the mass underneath created gelid traps. On sunny days, a yellowish epidermis might be discernible, but pilots had no fool-proof methods to judge its depth until grey blobs slammed against the aircraft and froze solid. Worse still, the skis became overloaded while taxiing, often resulting in the hypothetical glamour associated with manipulating the 'Grand Old Lady' evaporating. Everyone shovelled furiously, and in extreme situations, tramped clear pathways from which to take off; this occurred multiple times a day.

attitude. This enables a slow initial impact speed, which resulted in continuous snow-ski contact preventing the aircraft from becoming airborne again."

With a stall speed of 66mph, slow tail-low, full flap approaches with engines idling allowed a touchdown speed in the region of 74-80mph, and reduced landing runs to a minimum. Most pilots preferred a 'little bit of wheel' exposed for flotation and directional control when landing in deeper snow; on occasion, DC-3s arrived in as much as 18in (45cm) of snow with regular tyres. While perfect for short gravel

"During landing, the wheels are lowered within a speed range of 109-120kts. When they are down and locked, the skis are selected down," explained Ferguson. "The approach to the landing is made in the conventional manner. The throttles would be closed to assume a more or less three-point

runways, the wide low-pressure wheels kept the nose-heavy machine upright. Flight manuals claimed DC-3s could be landed tail-high with full brakes when the airspeed was above 40mph and the control column was held firmly back. During winter, drag from the snow slowed the

aircraft far more rapidly, meaning the brakes were rarely needed. Above all, pilot experience and technique counted. In Cole's case, his logbook disclosed more than 3,300 hours on type between 1980 and 1987. Despite a hard-earned understanding of idiosyncrasies associated with cold weather operations, frightening moments still became routine.

"We'd come in a bit slower and land almost three-point – ready to counteract any tendency to nose over. But we almost beaked her one time at Webequie Indian Reserve north of Lake Superior when we were on the ground," recalled Cole. "All I remember was looking straight down at the ice through the windshield. The props must have just about touched the ice – pure luck."

The 13,142 Douglas DC-3s built proved to be more than just thosands of rivets and a near mile of cabling. Keening gales, obscured surfaces and slush traps could not stop them or the stalwart crews who kept their machines airborne. With the need for Threes diminished today, just a few overlooked sets of skis remain, collecting corrosion behind company hangars or gathering dust in museums. Pilots, mechanics, and loaders, as well as the white-faced passengers who vomited on their aluminium floors, will always remember them. ●

LEFT Photographed in early winter 1946, Canadian Pacific Airlines DC-3 CF-CPV was fitted with wooden skis, thought to have been built by the Bick Pickle Company. Dubbed 'boards' by the pilots, they had no shock-absorbing rubber bungees, cords or cables
G H WURTELE

BELOW A ground handler turns his attention to digging out the frozen skis of an Austin Air DC-3 during the mid-1980s SAMUEL COLE

Audible
PROPAGANDA

The venerable Dakota played a key role in 'sky-shout' operations during the Malayan Emergency, as **Andrew Thomas** describes

The campaign against the Communist uprising in Malaya, known as 'The Emergency', began in June 1958 and lasted 12 long years. To counter the largely ethnic Chinese Communist Terrorists (CT) required British and Commonwealth security forces to innovate and develop new counter insurgency tactics. The CTs occupied areas of the jungle-covered Malay Peninsula; flushing them out became a deadly game of hide and seek where psychological warfare played its part. During 1951 and with the campaign at its height, one idea was to broadcast messages that could be heard by CTs who were otherwise unseen in the jungle, to either demoralise or induce them to surrender.

It was decided to fit an aircraft with loudspeakers to support the propaganda war. Initially the equipment was tested on an Auster Autocrat G-AJIZ, which carried a speaker beneath each wing and an amplifier in the cabin. Subsequently the equipment was fitted to several Auster AOP.6s, though the size of the aircraft limited its lifting capacity, so a larger platform was sought. The USAF lent a C-47 rigged with 'sky-shout' equipment for trials, which commenced in November 1952 and proved successful. Thus, in March 1953 the equipment was fitted into two RAF Valetta transports. However, this aircraft was unsuitable for the task due to its excessive engine noise, high stalling speed and inability to maintain the required orbit technique. However, the C-47 had a lower stalling speed and much reduced audibility in an operational configuration, so initially two, later three, surplus aircraft were ordered from stocks in the UK. In the interim, voice broadcast operations continued with the Austers of 1311 Flight, but one of the Valettas was withdrawn, being replaced by C-47B Dakota A65-72 loaned by the Royal Australian Air Force (RAAF). This allowed comparative trials to be flown during January 1954, which showed that the Dakota offered superior audibility and greater clarity with a signal that could be heard for two to three minutes when flown in a straight line.

Bulky equipment

On February 15, 1954, 1311 Flight at Kuala Lumpur became 267 Squadron under Sqn Ldr M E J Hickmott and it was mainly equipped with Pioneers for short-range transport work. The Austers and the two converted 'Daks' formed C Flight, though this was universally referred to as the 'Voice Flight.' Sadly, eight days later

Valetta WD160 crashed into Mount Ophir in Johore State, with the loss of the crew. As a result, the loan of the RAAF Dakota was extended to the beginning of June.

The three RAF Dakota C.4s were modified for 'sky-shouting' duties fitted with the loud speaking equipment for voice operations. However, it was both bulky and heavy, and included an internal Enfield Cub 5.6kVA diesel generator anchored to the floor by bolts and tie-downs. This provided 240V to power the four 500-watt amplifiers situated in each corner of the main cabin, and as many 500-watt speakers mounted on a beam (which could be jettisoned) attached beneath the fuselage; the speakers were usually painted bright yellow.

Broadcast equipment and the power supply occupied much of the interior, with the voice operator's station facing aft near the door. The speakers were angled to port at 45° downwards, which offered an effective range of 2,500 yards. From a designated datum the aircraft was flown in a left-hand circuit with an overlapping pattern, so that at 70kts a 30-second message could be heard in full, from a fixed position on the ground. The Tannoy operators were volunteers from among the flight's radio tradesmen and they also monitored the diesel generator. One of the operators, Sgt H W Batty, later received the British Empire Medal for his work with the unit. Tactically, the broadcasting aircraft would often follow an airstrike or ground engagement with security forces to 'encourage' the CTs to surrender. Most broadcast

flights lasted around four hours and were usually over uncharted territory, with one navigator plotting a previously unidentified jungle peak in northwest Malaya.

The first of the modified Dakotas, KP277 was issued to 267 Squadron's 'Voice Flight' on June 12, 1954 after which the Australian aircraft was returned. Airframe KJ955 was the next to arrive on July 15, followed by KJ810 on October 1. Echoing the RAF Gladiators on Malta during World War Two, they were named *Faith* (KP277), *Hope* (KJ955) and *Charity* (KJ810). The Dakotas soon began flying psychological warfare voice operations over the Malayan jungle and were used not just for 'sky-shout' broadcasting, but also for leaflet dropping as part of the intensive 'hearts and minds' campaign against the small hardcore of CTs and the uncommitted

ABOVE **Flames engulf Dakota C.4 KJ810 'Charity' after it crashed at Kuala Lumpur while attempting to take off with its elevator control locks still fitted** 209 SQN RECORDS

BELOW **The first RAF Dakota C.4 modified for voice operations was KP277 'Faith'. Note the four 'sky-shout' loudhailer speakers underneath the fuselage** MoD

>>>>

populace. It was the start of the flight's unconventional operations supporting the increasingly effective counter-insurgency campaign, with its three Dakotas and two Austers. During this first year, both types flew 600-plus voice sorties. The peak was in August when, during a 13-day special operation, 89 flights covered 400 targets.

Hailing Zones

Voice operations were flown so the intended target, a village, or a suspected terrorist hideout location, could hear the broadcast clearly… but not the aircraft. The proceedings commenced over the designated Hailing Zone at an ideal height of 2,500ft, as one pilot recalled: "The speakers faced outwards to port and were set to beam the audio at a set angle. The important thing was to keep the wings level to get the audio onto the intended target. The speakers' range was 2,000 yards to the left

and approximately 500 yards to the right. For a small visual target, a normal orbit could be used. [However], cloud and rain diffused the audio, making ground reception very poor."

The short tapes to be broadcast would be usually produced in the studios of Malaya Radio, recorded in various dialects such as Hakka, Mandarin, Malay, and Cantonese. The tapes would be delivered to the Voice Flight at Kuala Lumpur by Psychological Warfare Dept staff, together with maps showing the required Hailing Zones plotted. The aircraft would then be dispatched quickly to the supplied jungle coordinates.

This procedure was simplified for short-notice tasks when required, by recording a message in a voice booth in the flight HQ, or even on board the aircraft. The key was that any messages broadcast had to be short and contain true information, thus notifying Communist cadres of the deaths, or surrender of

> "…any messages broadcast had to be short and contain true information, thus notifying Communist cadres of the deaths, or surrender of comrades…"

comrades in various parts of Malaya. It was soon established from captured CTs that they never doubted information heard from a voice broadcast aircraft.

The Voice Flight was effectively an autonomous element within 267 Squadron and during 1955, Sqn Ldr T W G Godfrey became the squadron CO. Operations by

LEFT Dakota C.4 KJ955 'Hope' of the Voice Flight has yet to have its speakers refitted after major servicing

BELOW Two of the 267 Squadron Voice Flight Dakota C.4s sandwich an Auster at Kuala Lumpur in 1955

the Dakotas, with Austers covering shorter-ranged tasks, continued unabated as slowly, but surely, the Security Forces gained the upper hand. Ultimately, the CTs were driven into ever smaller and more remote bastions, known as 'black areas'.

The peak of psychological air warfare activity came during September 1955, when the CTs were offered a wide amnesty and during the year more than 900 hours of loudspeaker messages were broadcast throughout 922 sorties.

The situation steadily improved, in that by late 1958 the cessation of anti-terrorist operations in Johore led to the concentration of operations in the mountain areas of northern Malaya, resulting in Voice Flight's Austers being withdrawn. Then on November 1, 267 Squadron, by then under Sqn Ldr 'Mac' Hamilton, was re-numbered as 209 Squadron – though in reality little changed, with the unit's primary task remaining short-range transport with its Pioneer CC Mk.1s.

Thus, on January 19, 1959, Voice Flight Dakotas were detached to Bayan Lepas civil airport on Penang Island, to continue residual broadcast operations in support of the Security Forces in northern Perak and Kedah states. A few days earlier KP277 went to the Hong Kong Aircraft Engineering Company for maintenance, being replaced by KJ955 after its periodic servicing on January 22. Sadly, four days later at 1615hrs on January 26, the third aircraft, KJ810, crashed while

ABOVE **Voice Flight Dakota C.4 KP277 'Faith'** shows the proximity of the jungle-covered hills of northern Malaya, which were often encountered during broadcast operations

BELOW **Flt Lts Stanford and Taylor chat with groundcrew before another sortie in Dakota C.4 KP277,** after the Voice Flight had been absorbed by **52 Squadron** H G HAINES

taking off from Kuala Lumpur en route for Penang with its elevator locks still in place. It was destroyed in the subsequent fire but fortunately, the four-man crew escaped significant injury. The flight reduced to two aircraft until KP277 returned on March 16, 1959.

Final operations
Dakotas of the Voice Flight were an anomaly within 209 Squadron, so on November 2, 1959 it was transferred to the Valetta-equipped 52 Squadron based at Kuala Lumpur, commanded by Wg Cdr S R Dixon. The Voice

Flight continued operations from Penang under Flt Lt Harry Haynes, maintaining its standby at Bayas Lepas on call to the security forces 24 hours a day, seven days a week. Haynes recalled at the time: "To achieve successful ground reception the Dakota is flown in the configuration of speed – 70-75kts at 1,700 rpm with sufficient boost, about 24 to 25in. Wings must be kept level or the message which is 'beamed' by the set angle of the speakers will be thrown off target." He also commented on what the crews often had to endure: "Flying in the

turbulence of a Malayan afternoon in the mountains, one is constantly reminded that the stall is only a few knots on the minus side of the ASI needle, as the aircraft is caught by a sudden gust coming round a mountain peak."

After The Emergency ended on July 31, 1960 the two surviving broadcast Dakotas continued to be employed until late 1961. Dakota C.4 KJ955 was withdrawn on September 21 followed by KP277 on October 9, so bringing 'sky-shout' operations in Malaya to an end after more than 4,000 hours of broadcast during 4,500 sorties. ●

IN FOR THE
Long Haul

Dakotas joined the RAF in 1943 and one is still serving. **Ken Ellis** examines a quartet of veterans

Transports, particularly those relegated to second-line duties, tend to have long service lives. The ubiquitous Dakota proved to be so adaptable and robust that many air arms kept them going for decades. There was a time in the 1950s and 1960s when the saying, "the only replacement for a DC-3 is another DC-3" was a truism.

The military version of the pure airliner DC-3 was used by the USAAF as the C-47 Skytrain and C-53 Skytrooper. The C-47 was configured for freight or paratroopers while the C-53 was a 'straight' troop transport with a conventional side door. Just more than 800 DC-3s were built, the rest – 10,123 – were military airlifters. Additionally, Japan and the Soviet Union manufactured the type under licence.

Rapid Wind-Down

RAF and Commonwealth air arms called the Douglas twin the Dakota – named after the American Indian tribe and twin US states – but inevitably shortened it to 'Dak'. There were four British versions: the Mk.I based on the initial C-47, the Mk.II on the C-53, the Mk.III on the C-47A and the Mk.IV on the C-47B. Figures vary, but 1,915 were given RAF serial numbers and just over 1,000 of those were Mk.IIIs.

Dakotas first entered RAF service with 24 Squadron at Gibraltar in March 1943, on general transport duties. Deliveries peaked to support the D-Day landings and airborne actions as the Allies strode across Western Europe. It was obvious the type would be used in large numbers by the RAF in the immediate post-war years, but planners could never have envisaged just how much longevity the Dakota would achieve.

This series examines the final years and disposals of British military examples. Here, we zoom

"There are some things that only a Dakota can do and in June 1954 the type made a return to the front line"

in on four long-running RAF Daks (see panel for more data). It is worth pointing out that although some Dakotas wore red-white-blue roundels, strictly speaking they were not in the RAF; they served the test fleets of the Ministries of Aviation or Technology, for example the Royal Aircraft Establishment (RAE), or with contractors.

The intended successor to the type in the RAF was the Vickers Valetta, descended from the Wellington bomber. The first of 211 transport versions began to equip 204 Squadron at Kabrit, Egypt, in May 1949 and the subsequent

wind-down was rapid. Last to convert was 110 Squadron at Changi, Singapore, which shed its remaining Daks by April 1952.

Beyond this, Dakotas continued with training, other second-line tasks and test fleets. At Dishforth, North Yorkshire, 242 Operational Conversion Unit (OCU) found the type ideal to introduce pilots to transport flying. The last fatal RAF Dakota accident occurred on August 28, 1957 when the 242 OCU C.4 KN649 suffered an engine fire and plunged into fields near its base, killing all three on board.

Speaking Out

There are some things that only a Dakota can do and in June 1954 the type made a return to the front line. In Malaya, the long-running anti-insurgency conflict – calmly referred to as 'The Emergency' – had employed leaflet-dropping from the beginning of hostilities in 1948. To extend the psychological warfare, a C-47 equipped with a 'sky-shout' voice broadcast system was borrowed from the USAF and trialled in October 1952.

Two Valettas of the Changi-based Far East Transport Wing were

ABOVE Dakota C.4 KN457 in the RAF 50th anniversary static display at Abingdon, in June 1968 ROY BONSER

BELOW Dakota KN645 during its brief stay at the RAF Museum 'out-station' at Colerne, 1974 KEC

ABOVE **KN645 'flying' within the cavernous National Cold War Exhibition at Cosford**
KEN ELLLIS

Whitney Twin Wasp engines. A Dak was scrounged from the Royal Australian Air Force and fitted with gear from the surviving Valetta, while a trio of other airframes was readied in Britain.

At Kuala Lumpur, 267 Squadron had re-formed in February 1954 as a general duties unit, with Scottish Aviation Pioneers and Percival Pembrokes. The first 'sky-shout' Dakota C.4 arrived on June 12 and in January 1955 all three, named *Faith* (KP277), *Hope* (KJ955) and *Charity* (KJ810), were operational. These were flown by 267s 'C' Flight, which was universally known as the 'Voice Flight'.

During November 1958, the unit was re-numbered as 209 Squadron and the Voice Flight continued its task. On January 26, 1959 *Charity* took off from Kuala Lumpur with the elevators locked and the inevitable happened: it stalled and was wrecked, thankfully without injury to its crew. This was the last time an RAF Dakota was written off in a flying accident. Daks relinquished the 'sky-shout' role in 1959.

fitted with a similar system in July 1953. Tragically, one of these, C.1 WD160, hit a ridge near Tampin, southeast of Kuala Lumpur, on February 23, 1954, killing its crew of four. The loud-hailer Valettas were a disappointment; the noise from their Bristol Hercules engines mostly drowned out the propaganda messages and the accident brought that experiment to a close.

What was needed was the serene and almost stealth-like approach made by the Dakota's Pratt &

RIGHT **Long-nosed 'Mayfly', TS423 at Duxford in November 1979, shortly after arriving from Farnborough** KEC

RAF Dakota veterans

RAF serial	KN452	KN645	TS423	ZA947
US designation	C-47B-25-DK	C-47B-35-DK	C-47A-75-DL	C-47A-60-DL
USAAF serial	44-76391	44-77003	42-100884	42-24338
RAF designation	Mk.IV / C.4 [1]	Mk.IV / C.4	Mk.III / C.3	Mk.III
Built at [2]	Oklahoma City	Oklahoma City	Long Beach	Long Beach
Taken on RAF charge	Mar 27, 1945	May 18, 1945	Sep 2, 1944	May 1971 [3]
Struck off RAF charge	Jul 22, 1969	Jan 10, 1972	Dec 31, 1955 [4]	Still going!
Present owner	[5]	RAF Museum	Aces High Inc	BBMF
Location	[5]	Cosford	Dunsfold	Coningsby

Notes: [1] RAF designations switched from Roman numerals to Arabic in 1948. [2] Douglas plants at Oklahoma City, Oklahoma, and Long Beach, California. C-53 Skytroopers built at Santa Monica, California. [3] Accepted by the Royal Aircraft Establishment. [4] Transferred to Controller, Services (Air) for use by the Air Ministry test and trials fleet. [5] Last known to be operating in Singapore as N62303 circa 1977.

"KN645 was sumptuously furnished for VIPs with armchairs, a settee and a cocktail cabinet"

Desert Finale

Another 'hot spot' was the venue for the Dak's final frontline use: Khormaksar, Aden, for operations against dissidents in the southern Arabian Peninsula. Flying Scottish Aviation Twin Pioneers in support of army actions in the Radfan area, north of the city, 21 Squadron had reformed in June 1965, and a couple of Daks were enlisted to supplement the 'Twin Pins'. Also at Khormaksar was the Middle East Communications Squadron (MECS), another unit that appreciated the Dakota's attributes.

Following its adventures in Malaya, former 'sky-shout' Dak KJ955 *Hope* was issued to MECS in June 1964. It was blown up by a terrorist bomb while parked at Khormaksar on May 29, 1965 – thankfully, no one was hurt.

For the Nepalese portion of HM Queen Elizabeth's tour of the Indian sub-continent in January 1961, Daks KN645 and KN452 briefly joined the Queen's Flight. Within two months of this deployment, KN452 was on charge with MECS, transferring to 21 Squadron in August 1965. Its job done, 21 disbanded on September 15, 1967 and on November 6, KN452 was ferried to 5 Maintenance Unit (MU) at Kemble, Gloucestershire, to await its fate.

The following year, KN452 was in the limelight at Abingdon, Oxfordshire, having been moved by road and re-assembled to take its place in the vast static line-up arranged to celebrate the 50th anniversary of the RAF (see June 2018 *FlyPast*). Returned to Kemble, KN452 was offered for disposal and acquired by Shackleton Aviation at Coventry, Warwickshire, and placed on the British civil register as G-AXJU.

The following year *Juliet-Uniform* was bought by the Kenya Police Air Wing, registered 5Y-AKB, but was disposed of in 1974. In the late 1970s and American-registered as N62303, it was based in Singapore. Like many Dakotas, in its final days it just faded away.

FlyPast reader Brian Dunlop recalls his association with KN452: "When I arrived at the Station Flight in Gibraltar in 1958 I was asked if I knew anything about Dakotas. So, by ignoring the golden rule of never volunteering for anything, I was given the machine to look after. It was in VIP configuration with ten seats and wood-panelled walls.

"I spent the next couple of years flying around the 'Med' in it. We were even forced down by our friends the French in Oran at the height of the Algerian war, as we were suspected of carrying arms! It was a good serviceable aircraft although when the floor was taken up to fix a blocked galley sink line, it revealed a lot of coal dust from the Berlin airlift [serving with 30 Squadron].

"In the late 1960s, I was out of the RAF, flying for East African Airways in Nairobi. The Kenya Police Air Wing crashed its DC-3 and it was replaced by none other than KN452 – the serial showed through the paint!"

Top-Brass Runabout

Refreshingly painted in post-war 'silver', blue and white and 'flying' within the huge National Cold War Exhibition at the RAF Museum, Cosford, Shropshire, is the last Dak to serve with the RAF. Dakota Mk.III KN645 arrived in Britain on May 27, 1945. It was earmarked for communications use by the British Air Forces of Occupation the following month.

That November, KN645 was sumptuously furnished for VIPs with armchairs, a settee and a cocktail cabinet. Among the high-rankers who availed themselves of the Dakota's ambiance were: Marshal of the RAF Sir Sholto Douglas, Field Marshals Sir Bernard Montgomery, Archibald Wavell and General Sir Brian Robertson – all later elevated to the House of Lords.

After its time in Germany, mostly based at Bückeburg, in June 1951 KN645 was ferried to 12 MU at Silloth in Cumberland for storage. Its usefulness was far from over and it was back on a series of special assignments: Malta Communications Flight at Luqa (1954-1955), Supreme Headquarters Allied Powers in Europe Communications Flight – based at Northolt, Middlesex – and Fontainebleau in France (1955-1958 and 1961-1962). It was in Nepal with the Queen's Flight in January 1961, along with KN452.

Norwegian Outpost

From December 1962, KN645 joined Air Forces Northern Europe (AFNE). Based at Northolt and Gardermoen, Oslo, Norway, AFNE oversaw Britain's commitment to NATO's northern flank. The long commute across the North Sea determined that a rugged twin-engined type was needed and KN645 shared the task with C.4 KP208. On September 1, 1967 '208

was retired to 5 MU, leaving KN645 to soldier on.

A replacement was lined up for KN645, in the form of the twin turboprop Hawker Siddeley Andover C.1 XS637 – this machine being a mere three years old. The final official passenger sortie by an RAF Dakota was staged by KN645 from Oslo to Northolt on April 1, 1970. This ended 27 years of front and second-line RAF service by the type. Two days later, KN645 was ferried to Kemble for storage.

Meanwhile, KP208 had been gifted to the Airborne Forces Museum at Aldershot, Hampshire. After dusting down at Kemble, it was flown to Odiham, Hampshire on May 18, 1970 for dismantling ready for the road trip to the museum. Thus, KP208 carried out the last sortie under RAF aegis until ZA947 joined the Battle of Britain Memorial Flight (BBMF) in 1993.

With the occasional refurbishment, KP208 spent the next 39 years on external display at Aldershot. It moved in 2009, only to start another stint outside, 'guarding' 16 Air Assault Brigade at Merville Barracks, Colchester, Essex.

At Kemble, KN645 was transferred to the care of the RAF Museum on January 10, 1972. It was painted in camouflage to represent the machine flown during the Battle of Arnhem by Flt Lt David Lord, who was awarded a posthumous Victoria

Cross in 1944. The Dakota was taken by truck to the RAF Museum's 'out-station' at Colerne, Wiltshire on May 1, 1974. The following year it was on the road again, this time to Cosford: it was placed inside the Cold War hall in 2006.

Glider Snatcher

Despite having been on the US civil register since March 1998, well-known film and television facilities specialist Aces High's Dakota is still called 'G-DAKS' by British audiences, after its former UK identity. In September 2019, this venerable performer chalked up four decades with Aces High; this is a long-hauler with an intriguing history.

Two days before the end of 1943, this C-47A was handed over to the USAAF and on February 25, 1944 was on charge with the Ninth Air Force. Six days later, the 436th Troop Carrier Group settled in at Membury, Berkshire, busy working up for D-Day. The Skytrain is thought to have served with the group's 79th Troop Carrier Squadron. It was at this phase of its history that it gained battle damage repair patches on its undersides.

On September 2, 1944 it was transferred to the RAF, becoming Dakota Mk.III TS423 and issued to 1 Heavy Glider Servicing Unit (HGSU) at Netheravon, Wiltshire. This busy outfit prepared assault gliders and tug aircraft for airborne operations.

BELOW **With its new serial number and RAE 'Raspberry Ripple' colour scheme, ZA947 looks resplendent in 1984** KEC

Dakotas of 1 HGSU air-tested, collected and ferried Airspeed Horsas and Waco Hadrians to surrounding bases to await the call to duty. It is at this time TS423 was equipped with 'snatch' equipment to recover a glider on the ground without the tug needing to land (see last issue for more on this subject).

By autumn 1945, the Dakota was serving at Down Ampney, Gloucestershire with 436 'Elephant' Squadron, Royal Canadian Air Force (RCAF), carrying Allied personnel around Europe. At this point, TS423 could have joined the mass exodus of Dakotas back to American control, but instead it headed east, for the Station Flight at Gatow, Berlin, on March 20, 1946. The warhorse was retired to 44 MU at Edzell, Scotland, in September 1947 and readied for disposal.

Lightning Radar

The Soviets blockaded surface routes into the American, British and French sectors of Berlin from June 24, 1948. Answering the call, TS423 was placed in the hands of contractor Airwork at Gatwick, Sussex on August 26 and it was ready for duty on March 9 the next year.

The future for TS423 took a very different turn on August 16 when it was handed to major Dakota specialist Scottish Aviation at Prestwick, Scotland, to be turned into a test bed. A new elongated

> ## "TS423 was equipped with 'snatch' equipment to recover a glider on the ground without the tug needing to land"

nose section was the most obvious modification. By 1951, this extension terminated in a curved, glazed mounting. Some sources have referred to this as a 'gun turret', but it is believed it was used for optical weapon aiming, camera, or even searchlight experiments.

Dates are vague relating to its next alteration, with 1952 given as the earliest for the installation of a Ferranti Airborne Interception Radar and Pilot Attack Sight System (AIRPASS). This was being developed for the English Electric F23/49, which emerged as the awesome Lightning. The long nose on TS423 made it an ideal candidate to test AIRPASS' capabilities and it flew with the distinctive conical radome adopted by the Lightning.

On January 18, 1955, TS423 flew to Langley, Buckinghamshire for overhaul by Airwork. On the last day

of 1955 it was officially 'deposited' (handed over in paperwork at least) to Ferranti for operation in Scotland from Turnhouse (Edinburgh Airport) and West Freugh, near Stranraer. By this time the Dakota carried the name *Mayfly* on the nose – perhaps a sarcastic comment on its serviceability!

Scottish Aviation looked after the Ferranti Flying Unit's maintenance needs until October 1967, when *Mayfly* was to be found at West Malling, Kent, receiving attention from Shorts. It may have been at this point the 'needle' radome at the end of its nose was removed and replaced by a fairing. Certainly, by May 1969 this had been carried out as Marshall of Cambridge readied *Mayfly* for the RAE back at West Freugh.

Working alongside TS423 was 'KG661'. The RAE used these two for trials of sonobuoys – air droppable submarine detection equipment. Replaced by an Andover C.1 (probably XS646) in 1978, both were flown to the RAE headquarters at Farnborough, Hampshire.

Film Star

Mike Woodley, Aces High's leading light, discovered that the next likely 'home' for TS423 was the fire school at Catterick, Yorkshire. With very low airframe hours (around 3,000) there was plenty of life left in the veteran

the *Express* joined RAE's Transport Flight for general duties.

While at Farnborough, doubts were cast on 'KG661'. Examination of that airframe's service record discovered it was with 109 Operational Training Unit at Crosby-on-Eden (the present-day Carlisle Airport), Cumberland. The Mk.III had been written off on December 13, 1944 in a non-fatal take-off accident that left it a burnt hulk.

Enquires with Scottish Aviation revealed this machine had been delivered to the RCAF as 661 in September 1943. Its final years were spent in Europe, including a spell at Manston, Kent. In the early 1960s, it was based at Grostenquin in France with the RCAF's 109 Flight. Scottish looked after many RCAF assets and when 109 Flight disbanded in August 1963, Dakota 661 was ferried to Prestwick and stored.

While preparing it for the RAE, believing the digits '661' were part of an RAF serial, research showed that the prefix 'KG' was appropriate and the *second* 'KG661' was born. This anomaly could not be allowed to continue and in June 1979 the *Express* was given a serial in the then current RAF sequence, ZA947, a number that would look much more at home on the side of a Panavia Tornado.

After a major overhaul by Dakota specialist Air Atlantique at Coventry, Warwickshire, and a respray into camouflage at RAF Marham, Norfolk, ZA947 joined the BBMF at Coningsby, Lincolnshire, in June 1993. Its career has proven the adage: "You can wreck a 'Dak', but you can't wear it out!" ●

so Mike submitted a bid and it was accepted. On September 14, 1979, TS423 became G-DAKS on the British civil register and, 24 days later, it was ferried to Duxford, Cambridgeshire. During the winter months *Kilo-Sierra* was given a 'nose job', returning its profile back to the one it was 'born' with.

A new career as a media star kicked off in 1980 when it was given the first of many temporary colour schemes, as 'G-AGHY' *Vera Lynn* of 'Ruskin Air Services' for the Yorkshire TV series *Airline*, which was screened in 1982. In March 1998, the change was made to the US civil register, G-DAKS becoming N147DC. Based at North Weald, Essex from November 1985 and from 2008 at Dunsfold, Surrey, this old stager has an impressive credits list, more recent big-screen parts including *Red Tails* (2012) and *The Monuments Men* (2013) and it has been a firm favourite on the airshow circuit since 1980.

Identity Crisis

The need to provide a multi-engined 'tail-dragger' to prepare pilots for BBMF's Avro Lancaster B.I PA474, and help conserve the bomber's flying hours, coincided with the Parachute Regiment's wish to have a flying memorial to the airborne forces. This led in June 1993 to the RAF taking on charge an aircraft that was 50 years old – Dakota C.3 ZA947.

By 1970, the RAE at West Freugh was looking for a way of supplementing *Mayfly* and discovered that Scottish Aviation at Prestwick had a former RCAF example in store. This was duly acquired and it was handed over in May 1971 in RAF markings, wearing the serial 'KG661'. It was given the name *Portpatrick Express* after the coastal town used as a waypoint on sorties out of West Freugh.

Replaced by an Andover, *Mayfly* and *Portpatrick Express* were transferred to Farnborough. The former was put up for disposal, but

Puff the
MAGIC DRAGON

ABOVE RIGHT With a characteristic Vietnam-era protective wall to the parking area, this AC-47 awaits its next sortie. 'Spooky' artwork is evident on the nose MALCOLM V LOWE COLLECTION

BELOW RIGHT The C-47D 43-16369 repainted as 43-49770, the gunship in which Airman 1st Class John Levitow was a crew member when he saved the aircraft and crew through his heroic act. This C-47 is owned by the American Flight Museum of Topeka, **Kansas** FLY-BY-OWEN VIA BOB ARCHER

On the evening of Monday February 24, 1969, AC-47D 43-49770, call sign 'Spooky 71' of the 14th Air Commando Wing (ACW) took off from Bien Hoa Air Base, Republic of Vietnam (RVn) for a night combat air patrol. After more than four hours, pilot Maj Ken Carpenter was directed towards Viet Cong guerrillas attacking the giant Long Binh Army Post. The facility was the largest of its kind in the republic, and therefore a lucrative target for communist forces. As 'Spooky 71' headed towards Long Binh, the cockpit crew saw muzzle flashes. The aircraft was placed into an orbit, while the loadmasters opened the cargo door on the port side and prepared to launch magnesium flares, designed to float slowly to earth for three

minutes, while giving off a dazzling two million candlepower, illuminating the ground below. With no infra-red sensors to detect targets, flares were the most effective method of identifying the enemy forces below.

Understandably, the flares did not just illuminate the attackers, but also pinpointed the orbiting gunship. Despite the 7.62mm miniguns wreaking havoc on the ground, the Viet Cong were not going to let the opportunity of responding to a lucrative American target go unchallenged. Small arms fire from the ground hit the AC-47 in several places, but a mortar round that exploded when it hit the starboard wing, showering the fuselage with shrapnel, did the most damage. Small fragments of metal sliced through the aircraft's

skin, injuring five men including Airman 1st Class John Levitow. John had suffered more than 40 wounds, with one of his legs being partially paralysed. However, his instincts were to safeguard the other crew members. One colleague was laying unconscious close to the open doorway, and John struggled to move him to safety. It was then that John noticed one of the large Mk.24 flares with the safety pin removed and smoke pouring out, ready to ignite. Instinctively, he grabbed the flare and dragged it to the open door. With a super-human push, he ejected the flare, which ignited almost immediately. Mercifully, the actions of

During the 1960s, veteran Douglas Dakotas, in AC-47 gunship format, spearheaded an attack programme above the jungles and rugged terrain of South East Asia, as **Bob Archer** discovers

John saved the aircraft and the crew of seven.

While the extremely dangerous situation was unfolding in the cabin, Maj Carpenter regained control of the damaged aircraft, and banked away from the siege area, to make an emergency landing at nearby Bien Hoa. Once on the ground, the wounded men were taken to hospital. It was then that an inspection of the damage to the AC-47 revealed a huge hole in the wing where the mortar round had exploded. This, together with small arms fire had left some 3,500 holes in the aircraft.

The crew of 'Spooky 71' all recovered, including John Levitow, who was recommended to receive the Congressional Medal of Honor, the highest award that a US military serviceman can receive. John returned to his squadron and flew a further 20 combat missions. Additionally, the AC-47 was repaired by a team of expert sheet metal workers and technicians. On June 30, 1969, the aircraft was transferred to the RVn Air Force as part of the programme to boost the strength of indigenous forces, enabling the US military to gradually

BELOW **AC-47D 43-49499** at Tan Son Nhut in early 1966. The aircraft subsequently served with 14th ACW/SOW at many South Vietnamese air bases, but was destroyed at Phan Rang AB by a rocket attack on **August 29, 1968** DAVE MENARD VIA BOB ARCHER

USAF
operating units

Note: Air Commando Squadrons/Wings changed to Special Operations Squadrons/Wings on August 1, 1968.

Wing	Base	Date Active
1st ACW	Hurlburt Field, Florida	27/04/1962 - 14/01/1966
	England AFB, Louisiana	15/01/1966 - 15/07/1969
	Hurlburt Field	15/07/1969
		AC-47D 1965, 1967-69
3rd TFW	Bien Hoa AB, RVn	08/11/1965 - 15/03/1971
		AC-47D 1965-66
14th ACW	Nha Trang AB RVn	08/03/1966 - 15/10/1969
		AC-47D 1966-69
3rd ACS		
4th ACS plus A Flight Da Nang; B Flight Pleiku; C Flight Nha Trang; D Flight Bien Hoa; E Flight Binh Thuy		
14th ACS A Flight Nha Trang; B Flight Phan Rang; C Flight Bien Hoa; D Flight Binh Thuy		
432nd TRW	Udorn RTAFB, Thailand	18/09/1966 - 23/12/1975
		4th SOS AC-47D 1969-70
4410th CCTW	England AFB	25/08/1966 - 15/10/1969
4412th CCTS		AC-47D 1966 - circa 1972

withdraw from the region. The fate of the aircraft is unknown, but it was probably captured by the North Vietnamese when their forces swept across the south… subsequently reuniting the country under communist rule.

Project Tailchaser initiated the USAF aerial gunship programme in December 1962, organised at Wright-Patterson AFB, Ohio by the Aeronautical Systems Division (ASD). During the second half of 1963, Convair C-131B 53-7820 tested the

theory to prove that a target could be continually tracked while flying in a banked orbit. The pressing needs of the Vietnam War rekindled the programme, with a General Electric six-barrelled SUU-11A 7.62mm Minigun installed on the port side. By mid-1964 the C-131 was evaluated by the Air Proving Ground Center (APGC) at Eglin AFB, Florida, against targets on land and anchored in the Gulf of Mexico. The results were astounding, although the C-131 was not ideally suited to the task. Instead, the Douglas C-47 Dakota was selected primarily, as it was slow enough to hold the bank angle, and surplus airframes were available. While the C-131 was continuing tests, APGC C-47D 43-48462 had begun conversion with the ASD Flight Test Fabrication and Modification Division and began testing early in 1964. The Dakota featured two

SUU-11s protruding through open windows, with a third mounted in the doorway.

Tailored transformation

Due to the urgent requirement for the system, conversion was carried out in just a few weeks, with much of the hardware and equipment obtained from local sources outside of the usual supply chain. A brief evaluation followed, while concurrently two further airframes were converted for early field development. The C-47D 43-48579 was at Bien Hoa AB, RVn, in February 1964, followed in July by 43-48491. Both were employed to evaluate operations within the Vietnamese theatre. The first aircraft was trialled at a host of Vietnamese bases, before finally being retired in the USA. The second followed a similar career before joining

the RVnAF. All three retained the designation C-47D throughout.

The success of the test and evaluation programme resulted in six C-47s being budgeted for conversion to gunships. A further 20 soon followed. These were all modified by contractor Air International of Miami, Florida. Most were flown to South Vietnam for operations, although a small number were retained in the USA to convert crews.

On September 7, 1965, the 26 aircraft under conversion were

redesignated FC-47D. However, the fast jet community in South Vietnam was very unhappy with the F prefix, indicating Fighter; they considered the lumbering C-47 to be far removed from the mission they flew. Gradually the designation AC-47D was applied to 24 of these (two having been lost during combat operations in December 1965).

In total, 53 aircraft were configured as operational gunships for the USAF, not including the three test and development

LEFT **Two of the three miniguns mounted inside an AC-47D. Some AC-47s had two firing through open windows, and the third in the open doorway, while others were all mounted behind open windows** USAF VIA BOB ARCHER

LEFT **This airframe, 43-49516 of the 4th SOS, was a later conversion to AC-47D standard. It reportedly went to the RVnAF before transfer to Cambodia, and finally to Thailand** DAVE MENARD VIA BOB ARCHER

ABOVE **An FC-47D, 43-48801, taxiing at Miami Airport in September 1965, having completed conversion to gunship format by Air International. After serving in the USAF, it was transferred to the RVnAF on June 30, 1969** EMCS VIA BOB ARCHER

BELOW RIGHT **An aerial view of Tan Son Nhut Air Base, with some 30 Dakotas visible. Among these are several AC-47s** USAF VIA BOB ARCHER

airframes; 51 aircraft were designated as AC-47Ds with the new prefix being allocated between January 4, 1966 and January 18, 1968. All except four served with the RVn.

As the conversion programme got underway, the need for crews to man the aircraft had to be addressed. Those performing the gunship mission required two pilots (aircraft commander to fire the guns, co-pilot to fly the aircraft), a navigator (to corroborate targets), a flight engineer (to rectify any mechanical issues), a loadmaster (to arm and drop the flares), and two weapons technicians (to load and operate the guns). Training Detachment 8 of the 1st Air Commando Wing was formed at Forbes AFB, Kansas by August 29, 1965 to train all of these trades. Plans called for 11 conventional C-47s and four gunships, although a shortage of Miniguns meant just one of the latter was fully equipped. On December 1, 1965 aircrew training changed to a more established arrangement, with the formation

Tail Codes

Code	Squadron	Wing or Group and Base
EL	3rd ACS/SOS	14th ACW/SOW Nha Trang 01/05/1968 - 15/09/1969 Forward Operating Locations at Binh Thuy
	14th ACS	14th ACW Nha Trang 25/10/1967 - 01/05/1968
EN	4th ACS/SOS	14th ACW/SOW Nha Trang 08/03/1966 - 15/12/1969 FOLs at Bien Hoa, Da Nang, Pleiku, and Nakhon Phanom RTAFB.
ER	9th ACS/SOS	14th ACW/SOW Pleiku 9/1969 FOLs at Bien Hoa, Binh Tuy, Da Nang, Phu Cat, Tuy Hoa, and Udorn. Reported inactivated 29/02/1972.
IG	4412th CCTS	1st SOW England AFB 10/07/1968 -15/07/1969
	4410th CCTW	England AFB 15/07/1969 - 07/07/1970
	548th SOTS	4410th CCTW England AFB, 01/07/1970 - 15/09/1970
	4410th SOTG	England AFB, 15/09/1970 - 1/04/1972 Note - training South East Asian and Latin American AC-47 aircrew
IJ	548th SOTS	4410th SOTG England AFB, 01/04/1972 - by 01/07/1973
OS	4th SOS	432nd TRW Udorn 15/12/69 - 29/10/70 Flew three aircraft until 29/5/70

of the 4410th Combat Crew Training Squadron, 4410th Combat Crew Training Wing, at England AFB, Louisiana.

First to Vietnam

The initial aircraft completed the long ferry flight from Florida to Vietnam, where the 4th Air Commando Squadron (ACS) relocated from Forbes AFB to Tan Son Nhut AB, near Saigon on November 14, 1965. The first machine arrived without the miniguns, which were sent separately. Delays in the weapons delivery hindered combat operations beginning as planned. However, Miniguns began to arrive during December, enabling one or two aircraft to commence limited combat sorties. The subsequent increase in the number of aircraft delivered enabled gunships to be deployed to other RVn air bases. Those selected were close to areas that sustained repeated attacks by the Viet Cong and regular North Vietnamese forces. In addition, four FC-47s were deployed to Udorn Royal Thai AFB, Thailand for daylight armed reconnaissance operations over parts of Laos.

Unsurprisingly, the FC-47/AC-47s were quickly introduced into combat across much of South Vietnam, and in a limited manner over Laos. The last days of 1965 were extremely busy for the 4th ACS. Official figures state the squadron flew 277 combat missions, accumulating 1,441 flight hours, mostly during darkness, primarily to defend forts and villages from attack. More than 135,000 rounds of 7.62mm ammunition were expended, with some 105 Viet Cong being killed. Two FC-47Ds were lost during the period, although the first, 43-49492 was shot down while on a courier flight on December 17. The second was 45-1120 which crashed in Laos on December 24. The second loss was just a few hours before the Christmas bombing halt was due to be introduced.

The success of the gunships soon resulted in various nicknames being applied, and included 'Spooky', and 'Puff the Magic Dragon'. Indeed, the squadron began using the callsign 'Spooky', and an emblem of a ghostly figure was painted on the nose.

As 1966 opened, and the pause finished, the gunships returned to nightly operations. Aircraft began to be deployed to other air bases as

AC-47D
Aircraft

C-47D to FC-47D

Serial	Fate
43-49492	shot down 17/12/1965
45-1120	shot down 24/12/ 1965

C-47D to FC-47D / AC-47D

Serial	AC-47D Conversion	Fate
43-48356	04/01/1966	shot down 23/03/1967
43-48466	04/01/1966	MAP RVnAF?
43-48501	04/01/1966	MAP RThaiAF
43-48701	04/01/1966	MAP RVnAF
43-48801	28/02/1966	MAP RVnAF
43-48916	28/02/1966	MAP RVnAF
43-48925	28/02/1966	shot down 03/06/1966
43-49124	28/02/1966	shot down 08/01/1967
43-49268	28/02/1966	shot down 13/03/1966
43-49274	04/01/1966	destroyed 13/12/1968
43-49330	28/02/1966	destroyed 12/03/1968
43-49499	28/02/1966	destroyed 29/08/1968
43-49503	28/02/1966	MAP RVnAF
43-49546	28/02/1966	shot down 15/05/1966
44-76290	28/02/1966	shot down 09/03/1966
44-76370	28/02/1966	MAP RVnAF?
44-76394	28/02/1966	MAP RVnAF
44-76534	28/02/1966	shot down 28/03/1967
44-76542	28/02/1966	crashed 18/02/1967
44-76593	28/02/1966	MAP RVnAF
44-76606	28/02/1966	MAP RVnAF
44-76722	28/02/1966	MAP RVnAF
44-77263	04/01/1966	MAP RVnAF?
45-0919	28/02/1966	MAP RVnAF

C-47D to AC-47D

Serial	AC-47D Conversion	Fate
43-16065	09/06/1966	MAP RVnAF
43-16133	17/01/1968	MAP RVnAF
43-16159	09/06/1966	shot down 04/05/1968
43-16368	17/01/1968	MAP RVnAF
43-48263	30/08/1966	MAP RVnAF - Lao AF
43-48591	30/08/1966	shot down 02/10/1967
43-48686	30/08/1966	MAP RVnAF
43-48921	30/08/1966	destroyed 26/04/1967
43-48929	31/10/1967	MAP RVnAF
43-49010	17/01/1968	MAP RVnAF - Cambodian AF? RThaiAF
-		
43-49021	30/08/1966	shot down 01/09/1969
43-49211	17/01/1968	MAP RVnAF
43-49339	09/06/1966	MAP RVnAF
43-49421	09/06/1966	MAP RVnAF
43-49423	17/01/1968	MAP RVnAF?
43-49516	17/01/1968	MAP RVnAF? - Cambodian AF? RThaiAF
-		
43-49517	30/08/1966	MAP RVnAF
43-49770	31/10/1967	MAP RVnAF
43-49859	02/11/1967	shot down 14/02/1968
44-76207	30/08/1966	shot down 04/05/1968
44-76354	06/11/1967	MAP RVnAF
44-76625	18/01/1968	MAP RVnAF?
45-0927	09/06/1966	MAP RVnAF?
45-1047	18/01/1968	MAP RVnAF?
45-1057	31/10/1967	MAP RVnAF?
45-1117	30/08/1966	MAP RVnAF
45-1121	09/06/1966	MAP RVnAF?

RIGHT **A posed but nonetheless interesting image of a gunship being prepared for a sortie. Many thousands of rounds could be fired from an AC-47's three 7.62mm Miniguns during a typical operation. Note the ground covering, which was the 1960s equivalent of World War Two Pierced Steel Planking** USAF

flights were established to reduce the transit time to target areas. Among the bases housing small numbers were Binh Thuy, Da Nang and Pleiku. The squadron relocated to Nha Trang in May 1966, joining the 14th Air Commando Wing. While missions primarily involved close air support of small villages, the increasing number of aircraft enabled profiles to be expanded to include support of ground combat operations, armed reconnaissance, as well as control of air strikes by other aircraft types. This included directing other strike assets onto targets, as well as attacking the objectives themselves. Occasionally, the gunships were included in a mixed complement of aircraft in a coordinated offensive against larger concentrations of enemy forces.

Where possible, American ground troops liberated ancient forts as well as more modern constructions for headquarters in local areas.

All too often the enemy attacked these structures to try and kill the Americans, or at least force them to retreat. The commanders of these small to medium-sized concentrations of troops quickly appreciated the capabilities of

'Spooky'. gunships. As soon as the enemy began an assault, the requirement for assistance was sent up the chain of command, with an AC-47D being dispatched quickly. Once sufficient aircraft were in theatre, it was common for one or two to be airborne, with another on standby, ready to launch if necessary.

To ensure the gunship crew could determine the position of the enemy, in relation to the friendly troop concentrations, they were in direct contact with the local commander. All too frequently, the enemy were extremely close to US or RVn ground forces, requiring a high degree of accuracy by the gunship personnel. As stated, flares were launched through a tube which, once ignited, illuminated the ground and enabled the three miniguns to 'spray' the target area. Enemy forces were either killed or withdrew, resulting in the fort or village being saved from being overrun.

The inclination of the miniguns was usually 15° downwards, with the aircraft flown at a 30° bank angle, enabling the pilot to maintain orbit for a considerable time. The miniguns could fire up to 6,000 rounds per minute, although this was often reduced to 3,000 to extend time on station.

Into Laos

Whereas the majority of operations were above South Vietnam, occasionally there were requirements for AC-47s to respond to requests in Laos. Early in 1969, communist Pathet Lao insurgents, supported by North Vietnamese forces, captured pro-government areas. During mid-March, four 4th Special Operations Squadron

(4th SOS) 'Spooky' gunships were relocated to Udorn. The AC-47s were immediately in action, with one maintained on airborne alert, and a second on ground standby.

During October 1969, the 4th was planning to cease AC-47 operations, as larger Fairchild AC-119 'Shadow' and Lockheed AC-130A 'Spectre' gunships were arriving. However, the AC-47 was extremely busy right up until the final days. One of the last large-scale missions involved AC-47s above South Vietnam, close to the Cambodian border. For 30 days, gunships flew two missions per night, firing more than 400,000 rounds and launching 8,000 flares. The targets were the usual Viet Cong and North Vietnamese regulars. Seemingly, the attackers employed very heavy ground fire, requiring combat tactics to be altered by 'Spooky' crews. The aircraft were flown away from the target areas to reload the guns, while the cockpit crews learned to throttle back the engines to mask the sound and prevent the enemy from pinpointing the source.

As the phase-out of the AC-47 continued, surplus aircraft were transferred to the RVn and Laotian Air Forces. The final 4th SOS sortie took place on December 1, 1969, when 'Spooky 41' landed at Phan Rang AB. Withdrawn AC-47s were transferred away through the Military Assistance Program (MAP), with a final three going to Vietnam and eight to Laos. A further trio went to the 432nd Tactical

Reconnaissance Wing at Udorn. The 'Vietnamisation' programme involved the transfer of 30 USAF AC-47Ds to the RVnAF between July 1969 and July 1972, where they were known as 'Fire Dragons'. Due to its crews having operated C-47s in conventional roles for many years, and their familiarity with terrain, their use of gunships was extremely effective. The gradual increase in gunship operations enabled the USAF to cease flying AC-47s completely by year end.

Over four years, the nightly actions by the gunship community resulted in 19 AC-47s being lost. Apart from the two in 1965, mentioned earlier, four were lost in 1966, six in 1967, six more in 1968, and just one in 1969. Sadly, there were 92 fatalities.... But 'Spooky' had well and truly paved the way for gunship progression. ●

ABOVE **The classic layout of armament finally chosen for the AC-47 was three 7.62mm Miniguns, although some experimentation took place to perfect the arrangement. The official caption to this image states that it shows three MXU-470/A Minigun modules** JB VIA MALCOLM V LOWE

BELOW **A famous long exposure image, showing a 'Spooky' at work over South Vietnam, many such sorties being flown at night. The red lines are tracer rounds, which were just a small percentage of the total 7.62mm ordnance being fired** MALCOLM V LOWE COLLECTION

C-47

This past and present list is not exhaustive; due to the nature and longevity of the C-47, it is difficult to pinpoint every single user globally, especially where clandestine activity is considered.

MILITARY OPERATORS

*Denotes countries reported to have operated the type, but evidence is lacking

1 Angola
2 Argentina
3 Australia
4 Bangladesh*
5 Belgium
6 Benin
7 Biafra
8 Bolivia
9 Brazil
10 Burma
11 Cambodia/Kampuchia
12 Cameroon
13 Canada
14 Central African Republic
15 Chad
16 Chile
17 China
18 Colombia
19 Comoros
20 Republic of the Congo
21 Democratic Republic of Congo
22 Cuba
23 Czechoslovakia
24 Denmark

25 Dominican Republic
26 Ecuador
27 Egypt
28 El Salvador
29 Ethiopia
30 Finland
31 France
32 Gabon
33 Greece
34 Guatemala
35 Haiti
36 Honduras
37 Iceland*
38 India
39 Indonesia
40 Iran
41 Israel
42 Italy
43 Ivory Coast

44 Japan
45 Jordan
46 Katanga
47 Kenya*
48 Laos
49 Liberia
50 Libya
51 Madagascar
52 Malawi
53 Mali
54 Mauritania
55 Mexico
56 Morocco
57 Mozambique
58 Nepal

66 Oman
67 Pakistan
68 Panama
69 Papua New Guinea
70 Paraguay
71 Peru
72 Philippines
73 Poland
74 Portugal
75 Rhodesia
76 Rwanda
77 Saudi Arabia
78 Senegal
79 Somalia
80 South Africa

95 Togo
96 Turkey
97 Uganda
98 Upper Volta
99 Uruguay
100 United Kingdom
101 US
102 Venezuela
103 Vietnam
104 West Germany
105 Yemen
106 Yugoslavia
107 Zaire/Congo
108 Zambia
109 Zimbabwe

81 South Arabia/South Yemen
82 Southern Rhodesia
83 South Korea
84 South Vietnam
85 Soviet Union
86 Spain
87 Sri Lanka
88 Sudan
89 Sweden
90 Singapore*
91 Syria
92 Taiwan
93 Tanzania*
94 Thailand

59 Netherlands
60 Netherlands East Indies
61 New Zealand
62 Nicaragua
63 Niger
64 Nigeria
65 Norway

A Legend
REBORN

Few who witnessed Douglas' Commercial Model Three maiden flight from California's Santa Monica Airport on December 17, 1935, could have imagined it would still be flying - let alone earning a living - more than eight decades later.

Developed from the DC-2 and Douglas Sleeper Transport, what became known as the DC-3 featured a strengthened floor and a larger capacity. This formed the basis of the aeroplane that went on to become the mainstay of Allied transport efforts during World War Two – a machine that Gen Dwight D Eisenhower, Supreme Commander of the Allied Expeditionary Force in Europe, noted as one of the main reasons behind the Allies' victory. Today, just to the east of Wittman Regional Airport in Oshkosh, Wisconsin, USA there is a firm dedicated to transforming the DC-3/C-47 family into a modern-day legend by re-engineering the airframe and fitting turboprop engines. As a result, once old and tired Dakotas/Skytrains that plied their trade through war-torn skies are still being put to work well into the 21st century. That company is Basler.

Humble beginnings

In 1957, Warren Basler, a man raised on a farm just six miles south of the airport, established Basler Flight Service to complement his then new role as one of Wittman Regional's fixed base operators. During its formative years, Basler operated passenger and cargo charter services using a variety of types such as the Beech Bonanza, Aero Commander, various Beech twins, as well as examples of the DC-3, DC-4, and DC-6. However, as the company continued to grow, it naturally progressed towards aircraft maintenance – initially looking after its own fleet, before accepting other operators.

With services including restoration, interior rework and engine overhaul, it was a small step to modifying aircraft, in particular the venerable DC-3, with newer cost-effective turboprop powerplants and re-developing the airframes to bring them in line with the far more stringent safety standards required at the time.

Consequently, in 1988, Basler Turbo Conversions was formed to focus solely on the DC-3/C-47 family. The result? The incredible Basler BT-67. Tom Weigt, company president when the author visited in 2013, explained: "There is still demand for a '21st Century Dakota' around the world! Basler decided on the Douglas aircraft because of the availability of airframes, and the strength and reliability of the original structure. Initially

Ken Cothliff reveals how Wisconsin-based Basler Turbo Conversions, and its ubiquitous BT-67 programme continues to breathe new life into the venerable DC-3/C-47 family

the prototype was converted from an airframe found in Alaska that had been earning a living flying groups around the state's decidedly inhospitable terrain."

The rugged nature of the airfields and often rudimentary landing strips in that part of the world are a major factor in the Dakota being used 'up north' – as those readers familiar with the Discovery Channel's *Ice Pilots* will know.

Sixty-Plus

Every machine Basler acquires is first assessed for corrosion to ensure it is suitable for conversion, and to determine that there is *enough* aeroplane to work with. As you can imagine, given the type's worldwide service, aircraft come from every kind of climate. Subsequently, each requires different amounts of work. With customers charged a basic cost for the conversion – irrelevant of

issues and intricacies faced – the final contract value depends on the individual specification produced to meet the client's requirements. However, as time progresses and the airframes get older, more effort is often needed during the initial conversion phase. Subsequently, a converted 'Dak' needs about 80% of its airframe replacing. As well as the new material, the fuselage is extended by some 40in just in front of the wing, resulting in a larger cargo area. Similarly, the cockpit bulkhead is also moved forward 60in. With the fuselage stripped to its original specification, every component is checked and changed if necessary, while new and improved fuel, electrical and hydraulic systems are fitted. Likewise, the wings are scrupulously assessed and modified in accordance with the customer's specification before gaining new leading edges, metal control

surfaces and squared-off wingtips – the latter to improve low-speed handling. In addition to the type's wide fuselage and large cargo door, one of the original airframe's other strengths is the joint between the outer and inner wing sections – more than 200 bolts hold these together, eliminating the need for a full width, tip-to-tip main spar.

At the time of my visit, the firm was in the process of converting its 60th example of Douglas' legendary type, while its 61st candidate sat nearby at the very beginning of its transformation from Dakota to BT-67. Now, seven years on, airframes 68 (N1350A – a former USAAF and Spanish Air Force machine) and 69 (N941AT – an ex-USAF and Astro Airways aeroplane) are in the shop.

From the beginning the firm has utilised Pratt & Whitney's (P&W) 1,220hp PT6A-67AR as its engine of choice. Despite being an earlier

ABOVE **With Basler producing on average just two BT-67s a year, the company cannot rely on outside vendors. As a result, it has developed the capability to manufacture the 6,500-plus parts needed for each conversion in-house** KEN COTHLIFF

BELOW **Its ability to operate from some of the world's remotest climes is just one of the key attributes that makes the BT-67 a leading light in its class. Here three ski-equipped examples from Kenn Borek Air await their next journeys. Capable of carrying 18 passengers, the type has a maximum range of 12 hours or 2,300 miles** BASLER

BASLER BT-67 OPTIONS

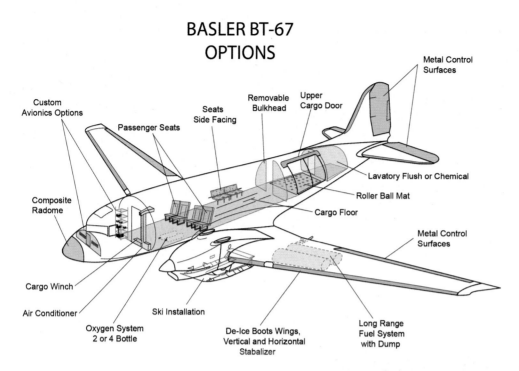

Labels: Custom Avionics Options · Passenger Seats · Seats Side Facing · Removable Bulkhead · Upper Cargo Door · Metal Control Surfaces · Lavatory Flush or Chemical · Roller Ball Mat · Cargo Floor · Metal Control Surfaces · Composite Radome · Cargo Winch · Air Conditioner · Oxygen System 2 or 4 Bottle · Ski Installation · De-Ice Boots Wings, Vertical and Horizontal Stabalizer · Long Range Fuel System with Dump

to meet our requirements for the foreseeable future – which makes it not worthwhile considering any other types such as the Convair 240 series."

While most of the converted aircraft are supplied with standard undercarriage, those slated for snow/ice operations are equipped with a specially designed retractable ski/wheel arrangement, as well as heat blankets for the engine, plus extra batteries, and hydraulics. Although several examples of the DC-3/C-47 were fitted with floats, Basler has never considered this an option as it would cause a major reduction in the amount it could carry, and result in an overly complex airframe modification.

Depending on what is required by the client, delivery normally

ABOVE **A graphic demonstrating the options available to BT-67 customers** BASLER

RIGHT **Seen in Basler's workshop during the author's 2013 visit, airframe 61 has since been converted into a BT-67. Registered C-FGCX, it was delivered to Canada's Kenn Borek Air in early 2015. Originally built as a C-47A by Douglas sometime in 1942, this former USAAF and Israeli Defense Force machine arrived in Wisconsin in April 2004** KEN COTHLIFF

example of the turboprop with its basic design dating to the late 1950s, it is known for incredible reliability. Fitted with a five-bladed Hartzell propeller and de-icing systems, it is considerably longer than the type's traditional P&W R-1830 Twin Wasp radial engine, which requires the original wing centre section and engine mounts to be strengthened, as well as specially produced composite nacelles. As a result, these improvements make the aircraft both quieter and faster, with its cruise speed sitting around 241mph – an increase of 24% over the piston-powered DC-3. In parallel, these changes also mean the converted Dakota has a far greater maximum take-off weight of 28,750lb. Subsequently, it has a payload capacity of some 4,000lb, an increase of 43% over Douglas' original design.

Going digital

As expected, the cockpit incorporates many changes – in particular, modern avionics (including the likes of a digital flight data recorder and autopilot), communication systems and navigation aids. Although, it should be noted that, despite bringing the type into the 21st century, Basler doesn't intend to install a so-called 'glass cockpit' in the BT-67 as they can be very demanding... and make

training on the type considerably more difficult. This is particularly relevant when many of these aeroplanes are operated across Third World countries.

As it stands, Basler has limited its conversions to just the DC-3/C-47 family, and although it has a 'Super Dakota' airframe on site (N100BF), it's deemed this variant of the type is not suitable for regeneration. Likewise, license-built examples such as the Soviet Union's Lisunov Li-2 (see *Soviet Stablemate*, pages 46-51) and Japan's Nakajima L2D have not been considered either. As Warren Basler often lamented: "The DC-3 was a beautiful, stable, and virtually indestructible airframe going to waste. We realised that... and by 'turbinising' and modernising it, it would go on for many years." Continuing, Tom explained: "There are more than enough DC-3 airframes around

> ## "...a converted 'Dak' needs about 80% of its airframe replacing"

takes between 8-12 months, with a typical conversion taking between 35,000-50,000 man hours. However, with Basler boasting a healthy backlog and order book, the waiting times, are well over a year as it currently stands. It should be noted that the firm does not hold converted machines in 'stock' – each is produced as it is needed, with either the customer supplying the airframe or Basler sourcing a suitable example.

LEFT May 5, 2010: The crew of BT-67 N923H releases dispersant off the shore of Louisiana to contain oil seeping from the infamous mobile offshore drilling unit, Deepwater Horizon, which exploded on April 20, 2010. A former USAAF machine, the aircraft is operated by Airborne Support on behalf of Clean Gulf Associates BASLER

BELOW Groundcrew carefully pump dispersant into N923H's tanks at Houma, prior to a sortie in response to the Deepwater Horizon disaster. Note the spray bar visible under the wing's trailing edge PO 3RD CLASS STEPHEN LEHMANN-USCG

However, the market is constantly changing, especially with civilian outfits operating on behalf of governments in areas such as scientific and environmental analysis work… to which the BT-67 is very much suited. Survey packages can include Magnetic Anomaly Detector booms and numerous underwing hardpoints and pylons, along with a multitude of sensors that feed back to equipment and apparatus in the cabin powered by a 400-amp generator. With several geographical/scientific research institutes and groups requiring the use of Light Detection and Ranging (LIDAR, sometimes also referred to as active laser scanning) the aircraft can be adapted with a composite radome, and openings in its belly and roof. Military options include seating for up to 40 troops/parachutists, static lines for the latter, covert lighting, forward looking infra-red, a night vision goggle compatible cockpit/cabin, countermeasures, and armour throughout.

At the time of writing – amid the ongoing COVID-19 pandemic – Basler is currently converting its 68th and 69th aircraft, with number 70, which has already sold, awaiting its turn. Joe Varkoly, the current company president, revealed: "We have 15 fuselages and airframes in storage, which is sufficient for the next seven or eight years, at a rate of two conversions a year." Besides manufacturing new BT-67s, Basler also offers support and maintenance packages. While long-term operators such as the Fuerza Aérea Colombiana (Columbian Air Force) – see *Phantoms over the Jungle*, pages 52-59 – carry out their own engineering schedules, smaller users including Northwest Africa's Mauritania, opt to return their aircraft to Oshkosh for deeper maintenance. Although phased

ABOVE **As part of its conversion, the aircraft's original fabric-covered flying controls are replaced with metal examples** KEN COTHLIFF

ABOVE RIGHT **Seen while supporting an Antarctic expedition, this BT-67 (C-GAWI 'Polar 5') is operated by Europe's sole user of the type – Germany's Alfred Wegener Institute for Polar and Marine Research** BASLER

BELOW RIGHT **Devoid of all markings, this is one of two BT-67s leased by the US Navy from Maryland-based firm AIRtec. However, their role is classified** BASLER

inspections are used, there is no dedicated time or hours, as those returning to the US operate across diverse environments and climates, meaning each will require differing levels of attention.

Turbo-Dak takeover

Recent deliveries include airframe 61, C-FGCX (a former USAAF and Israeli Defense Force machine) to the Polar Research Institute of China. Operated by type specialist Kenn Borek Air of Canada, it is used for arctic exploration. As well as airframe 60 (C-FKGL – an ex-USAAF and US Navy aeroplane), the firm's 63rd conversion (C-FKAL - a former USAAF and RAF example) joined Canadian charter, passenger, and cargo carrier Air Cargo North. However, both were involved in non-fatal accidents last year, but are said to be repairable.

With airframe 64 (N167BT) and 65 (N141PR) modified for LIDAR work, they were delivered to Maryland-based AIRtec, to provide critical airborne services such as range safety, maritime patrol, and airborne telemetry to government and science customers. Similarly, AIRtec took delivery of airframes 66 and 67. Leased by the US Navy, they wear a plain grey colour scheme marked solely with their registrations – N161PR and N181PR, respectively. However, the exact nature of their role and mission is classified.

So far, the only UK interest in the type has been from the British Antarctic Survey – although it only leases the aircraft from Kenn Borek Air. That said, the only true European user at present is the Alfred Wegener Institute for Polar and Marine Research based at

Bremerhaven, northern Germany. Operating two examples, C-GAWI 'Polar 5' and C-GHGF 'Polar 6' (Basler's 50th and 56th conversions respectively), the aircraft regularly undertake survey work across Europe and the Arctic.

With several examples modified with a dispersant aerial application system – better known as a spray bar – one of their primary roles is to counter oil spills. One such operator using this system is Airborne Support based at Houma in Louisiana, which deployed N932H – the 53rd aircraft converted – in response to the Deepwater Horizon oil rig disaster in the Gulf of Mexico during April 2010. Using a similar approach, several BT-67s have been tested in the aerial firefighting role. While many organisations tasked with this perilous mission

Service uses the type in this role, as well as others – including hauling cargo and even relocating animals. As well as Columbia's gunships, armed versions of the BT-67 have been employed by the air forces of Guatemala, El Salvador, and South Africa – the latter being one of the world's last major DC-3 operators.

If anything, the words of Basler's late founder, Warren Basler are the perfect closing for this feature: "For years, the aviation industry had been looking for a replacement for this rugged and reliable aircraft… at Basler Turbo Conversions, we're building it!" While this feature barely scratches the surface of the BT-67's flexibility and the wider Basler story in keeping the venerable type as a world leading asset, it does help prove the old adage 'the only replacement for a DC-3 is another DC-3!' ●

rely on vintage types such as Grumman's S-2 Tracker and Lockheed's P-2V Neptune, there is a 'kit' available to allow the BT-67 to be rapidly converted in just 20 minutes if urgently required. However, following several high-profile losses involving the likes of a Lockheed C-130 Hercules and a converted Consolidated Privateer among others, it has been recognised by many that much more modern platforms are required for this task – again, Basler's BT-67 airframe is well suited. As such the US Forest

Soviet
STABLEMATE

A successful lookalike of the DC-3/C-47 was produced in the Soviet Union as the Lisunov Li-2. **Malcolm V Lowe** relates the story of this much-used military and civil transport

ABOVE RIGHT The restoration to airworthy condition by the Goldtimer Foundation of Li-2 HA-LIX was completed in September 2001, when the aircraft made its first post-restoration flight. Its construction number is 18433209, meaning it was made by Factory 84, and it flew with the Hungarian flag-carrier airline MALÉV for part of its life
MALCOLM V LOWE

Under specific Lease-Lend arrangements between the US and Soviet Union during World War Two, the latter received a considerable number of C-47 airframes. These substantially added to the Soviets' limited transport assets… but there was a twist in the tale, because by 1941 the Soviet Union already had a DC-3/C-47 equivalent in production. Initially designated PS-84, it was the similar but also quite different Lisunov Li-2.

Unusual allies

It is often overlooked that there was considerable interaction between the US and the Soviet Union during the 1930s. Even though the two countries were potential adversaries and a world apart ideologically, this coming together worked very well. It included collaboration for such areas as motor vehicles, aero engines, and aircraft types. The latter included the granting of a licence to build the DC-3 in the Soviet Union.

The appearance of the DC line of airliners from Douglas created immense interest in many countries during the 1930s, and the Soviet Union was no exception; steps were taken to obtain a manufacturing licence to mass produce the type there. A batch of early DC-3 airliners was also bought for the Soviet state airline Aeroflot. The granting of a licence to build the type in the Soviet Union came to fruition with almost alarming speed, Douglas seeing the potential of gaining much needed finance from the growing interest in the DC-3/DST formula – even if it meant working with very strange bedfellows.

The details having been settled, several Soviet engineers visited the Douglas factories to begin the process of 'Sovietisation' of the basic design. In

fact, from the start it was obvious that the Soviet licence-building of the DC-3 was going to be more of a case of 'based on' rather than 'identical to'. The Soviets planned to perform significant modifications to the DC-3 layout, specifically the DC-3-196 formula, including a slight alteration to the wingspan, while a noticeable change was to make access to the fuselage for passengers principally from the starboard, rather than the port side, with significantly altered door

designs on both sides. It was also intended to power the new Soviet version with indigenous engines – although the chosen design, the Shvetsov M-62 (later ASh-62) air-cooled radial engine, was itself based on an American powerplant, the Wright R-1820 Cyclone, which had also been manufactured in the Soviet Union as the M-25.

The Soviet derivative of the DC-3 was given the

designation PS-84. The 'PS' stood in Russian for passenger aircraft. It was intended for manufacture to be undertaken at one of the Soviet Union's aircraft plants, namely the state factory numbered 84. At that time, the aviation industry in the Soviet Union was organised along quite different lines compared

BELOW Winter-camouflaged Li-2 '4026' fitted with a dorsal mid-upper turret. The Li-2 was of overwhelming importance to Soviet forces during the Great Patriotic War, although its contribution is often overshadowed by better-known frontline types NIKOLAI BARANOV COLLECTION

to European and US aircraft manufacturers and continues as such today.

Important among the Soviet technicians working in the US on the project was Vladimir Myasishchev, a talented engineer who, following World War Two, would head a design bureau responsible for the creation of the M-4 jet-powered strategic bomber. However, in the dictatorial and paranoiac atmosphere of the Stalin-led 1930s Soviet Union, Myasishchev was arrested and imprisoned during 1938 even though he had done nothing wrong. The project was therefore eventually named after Boris Lisunov, the engineer who was also working on the Sovietisation and series production of the DC-3; the type designation was changed because of this during September 1942 from PS-84 to Lisunov Li-2 – although the Soviet forces employing the type only started to refer to it uniformly as the Li-2 in 1943.

Making the DC-3 suitable for Soviet construction was a considerable undertaking. All dimensions had to be converted from US calculations to metric, the Shvetsov powerplants needed integrating and entirely new engine mounts were designed. It was also found that Soviet-manufactured metal for the stressed skin construction was of a different gauge compared to US standards.

The first aircraft was apparently completed in the Soviet Union during 1938, although the date

is unconfirmed. Built from a kit of parts supplied by Douglas and based on the DC-3-196 version, it is believed to have had the US construction number 2034. This first example, and most of the following handful also made from parts predominantly supplied by Douglas, were powered by Wright SGR-1820-G2 engines of US manufacture.

The first aircraft underwent state trials and obviously passed these because full-scale production of the true Soviet PS-84 led to several thousand airframes being completed. Construction was undertaken predominantly by Factory 84 at Khimki (a new town on the northwest outskirts of Moscow), and (in smaller numbers) Factory 124 at Kazan.

Aeroflot debut
What appears to have been the first fully Soviet example, with M-62 engines and roughly built to the intended PS-84 standard, was CCCP-L3404. This aircraft was registered during September

1939 (although it was possibly completed earlier than that) and is recorded as serving with the Soviet state airline Aeroflot during 1940. However, details of the early PS-84 airframes are very sketchy, and Soviet documents of the time, especially those giving the date of civil registration, are notoriously unreliable.

Nevertheless, the type was in full-scale production when the Soviet Union was invaded by Germany (Operation Barbarossa) on June 22, 1941. Germany's incredible and unprecedented

The manufacture of the PS-84 was no exception. Khimki's factory was closed and the whole operation sent by road and rail to the east, the destination being Tashkent (this Central Asian city is the capital of today's Uzbekistan). Airframes were being completed as the factory was closing, the final machine being recorded on October 18, 1941. The first completed PS-84 at the new location was rolled out during early January 1942.

The usefulness of the Li-2 was underlined by the number of different but related versions

of this version are believed to have also had an internal weapons bay for additional stores. On most, but not all, examples of the bomber version a dorsal mid-upper turret was fitted that could mount a single machine gun. There is evidence that some Li-2 airframes specifically used for transport were also fitted with the turret, to ensure a measure of self-protection if flying alone and unescorted.

Many versions

In addition, various other marks of PS-84/Li-2 existed, for

advances over vast areas of Soviet territory in the following months led to a rapid and massive programme of relocation of factories and heavy industry, away from the advancing front lines. Hundreds of major factories, and thousands of workers, were quickly moved further east to keep them away from the German forces. This allowed them to continue munitions production for the Soviet military without fear of being bombed or overrun.

eventually produced. The initial PS-84 transport was for civil and later military passenger use – and could be employed for cargo or a mixed load as a true utility aircraft, but it was joined by several different versions. The most significant was a derivative known in the West as the Li-2K (also sometimes referred to in error as the Li-2T), which gave the type a more warlike role. This was an armed transport and bomber, able to carry up to some 2,204lb of bombs externally; several examples

medical evacuation, training, and other roles including aerial photography/mapping and weather reconnaissance or research.

The end of World War Two was by no means the conclusion of the Li-2 story. In fact, the type remained in production until at least 1953, post-war identified designations being Li-2P for passenger airframes and Li-2T for cargo/passenger/troop carrying. These new examples were mainly constructed by Factory 126 at Komsomolsk-on-Amur, and by the original Factory 84 in its post-war guise. This happened despite a new airliner design intended to replace the Li-2 making its first flight during 1945 and having entered full-scale production soon after. It was the twin-engined Ilyushin Il-12, itself soon superseded by the Il-14, but the Li-2 soldiered on despite these newer designs.

The exact number of PS-84/Li-2 airframes manufactured is open to considerable debate and very wide interpretation. Soviet figures have suggested that 2,258 PS-84/Li-2 of all versions had been built by the end of World War Two. However, the post-war manufacture considerably

>>>>>

bolstered this number, leading to some sources claiming that 6,000-plus were eventually completed. However, more recent research suggests the total is less than this, with various figures that include 4,937, 4,924, 4,863, and 4,561.

Widespread service

Such was the pressing need for the PS-84 that the type entered service with the Soviet state airline Aeroflot almost immediately,

Lisunov PS-84/Li-2 (passenger transport) Specifications

Powerplant	2 × Shvetsov ASh-62IR nine-cylinder air-cooled radial piston engines, approximately (1,000hp) 746kW each for take-off
Crew	4
Passengers	up to 24
Length	64ft 5 3/4in (19.65m)
Wingspan	94ft 6 1/2in (28.81m)
Empty weight	16,149lb (7,325kg)
Max take-off weight	24,030lb (10,900kg)
Performance	
Maximum speed	198mph (318km/h) at 6,562ft (2,000m)
Range	1,553 miles (2,500km)
Service ceiling	19,685ft
Armament	None (see text)

Note: This information was kindly provided by the Goldtimer Foundation, operator of the airworthy Li-2 HA-LIX, and the Letecké Muzeum at Kbely, Czech Republic.

> "...the type continued to play its part in the Soviet military during the initial stages of the Cold War"

several aircraft being allocated during 1939-40 as production was only just gearing up to full capacity. The type was used at once to considerably expand the air routes across the vast Soviet Union in a way that had not been possible previously, alongside the DC-3 examples that had been bought 'off the shelf' from Douglas for the same purpose. The type was therefore in service at the time of Barbarossa.

The subsequent importance of the PS-84/Li-2 to the Soviet war effort cannot be overemphasised. Although the type receives little attention in Western histories of the air war over the Soviet Union, it was a vital transport aircraft that served with distinction through what the Russians refer to as the

'Great Patriotic War' of 1941-45. The type was used as a troop transport/ paratroop carrier and cargo aircraft, bomber, reconnaissance platform, ambulance, and trainer. It therefore performed frontline functions such as bombing, which the US C-47 was not required to do.

Following World War Two, the type continued to play its part in the Soviet military during the initial stages of the Cold War. It therefore received the attentions of NATO codenaming personnel, who gave the Li-2 family the reporting moniker 'Cab'. A significant role performed by some Li-2 transports was support and re-supply for Soviet Polar explorations, for example the Soviet drifting Polar station SP-3, and an Arctic expedition during 1954.

Foreign success

The type was also widely 'exported' as a military transport to countries under Soviet influence in Central and Eastern Europe, as well as

LEFT The Li-2 was much used for Polar flying and exploration, as demonstrated by this example. Note the ski undercarriage, and the shuttered frontage to the engine cowlings… a necessary feature for flying in extreme cold MALCOLM V LOWE COLLECTION

BELOW An image of true 1950s nostalgia: passengers embark on an Aeroflot Li-2, CCCP-L4850, at Kiev-Zhulyany airfield (now Kiev's international airport). This Li-2 flew throughout the 1950s, finally being struck off charge as airframe time-expired in November 1960 MALCOLM V LOWE COLLECTION

further afield with states friendly towards the Soviet Union.

Among the Eastern Bloc 'export' customers for the Li-2 was Czechoslovakia. This Central European country was also a major user of the C-47. In Yugoslavia, a true one-off was created by the re-engining of some Li-2 transports with US Pratt & Whitney R-1830 Twin Wasp radials, leading to an unofficial designation Li-3.

In the same way that the C-47 continued in military use during the 1960s in what became the Vietnam War, the Li-2 was also present in the region. During the 1960s, Soviet manned Li-2s were used for a variety of purposes, including covert work in Laos with Laotian-marked airframes, and the support of North Vietnam.

Li-2s continued in 'civilian' service following World War Two in considerable numbers, bolstered by post-war production of the type. Additional to extensive use by Aeroflot in the Soviet Union, the Li-2 was widely exported to countries within the post-1945 Soviet sphere of influence. Thus, the airliner proved to be a useful start-up type for several companies, in being an ideal short-haul regional and internal transport, both for passengers and cargo; it also flew on many shorter-range international services. Airlines such as LOT in Poland, MALÉV in Hungary, and Romania's TAROM found the Li-2 useful for many of their short- to medium-haul routes. In those days, medium-range journeys were considerably shorter than the equivalents flown by current jet airliners, but in the late 1940s and 1950s the Li-2 was a worthy workhorse. ●

Thanks to various friends and historians in the Czech Republic, Hungary, and Russia for specific details, including Csaba Bordács, Nikolai Baranov and Sergey Yakunin. Note: For ease of understanding, where possible, Latinised versions of Russian spelling/Cyrillic lettering have been used.

Phantoms

OVER THE JUNGLE

Colombia is the country with the longest internal conflict in the Americas... a war against communist guerrillas that started in 1964, but with its roots in the 1940s. Since the late 1980s, FARC and ELN guerrillas allied themselves to drug traffickers, who financed them, until being a direct component of drug production today. The guerrillas and other illegal groups are also currently undertaking illegal mining – a growing problem in Latin American jungles.

In response, the Colombian Air Force (Fuerza Aérea Colombiana, FAC) developed a capable counter-insurgency force, especially from the late 1980s, with helicopters and light aircraft, prosecuting what could be viewed as a modern version of the Vietnam War. Some of the aircraft types are even the same, albeit much modernised, such as Bell's Huey helicopter, Rockwell OV-10 Bronco and the AC-47T Fantasma, the most modern extant version of the famous AC-47 employed in South East Asia.

The FAC has operated the Douglas C-47 since 1944, but mostly just for transport. Colombia's difficult mountain and jungle topography, where aircraft needed to operate from unpaved runways, in hot weather and sometimes very high airfields, made the rugged C-47 an ideal choice. It was also cheap and reliable to fly. Because of this, they have operated for a very long time and Colombia still has the world's largest fleet of Douglas DC-3s on commercial service (see pages 110-114).

Gunships

As the war against the guerrillas became longer and more embittered, in the 1980s the FAC decided to modernise its fleet, developing plans to acquire Black Hawk helicopters, OV-10 Broncos, Embraer Tucanos, intelligence aircraft and many other types. In 1986 it was decided to modify some of the then remaining C-47s as gunships, using the experience obtained by the USAF and South Vietnam Air Force in Vietnam, and being similar to C-47s obtained by El Salvador to fight guerrillas in that country.

Santiago Rivas details how the Colombian Air Force still uses the Douglas AC-47 gunship, in its Basler BT-67 form, to tackle guerrillas and fight crime

With the help of the US government, in 1987 the first two airframes (FAC 1681 and 1686) were modified with three Browning M3 .50 cal machine guns. They also received new navigation and communications equipment, and an old sight taken from the Lockheed T-33, which was mounted on the port cockpit to help fire the weapons at a 25° angle. Flares of the LUU-2D/B variety were also employed for night illumination, and the first window of the rear cabin was removed, making way for an air intake, which helped to purge fumes and smoke from the weapons, exiting through the main door.

The two gunships were immediately successful, so other airframes – FAC 1650, 1652 and

1654 – were duly modified, but the age of the C-47 became evident when on August 30, 1988, '1650 had an accident while flying between Villavicencio and Girardot, killing all the occupants. Also, these aircraft lacked efficient equipment to operate at night, as the sight was only really designed for operations in daylight. Until then, for nocturnal sorties, targets were just illuminated with the flares.

A decision was taken to further improve the AC-47s by converting them to turboprop power... a product offered solely by Basler Turbo Conversions of Winsconsin (see pages 56-61), which also includes structural modifications, a longer fuselage and other changes, to becoming the BT-67,with Pratt

& Whitney PT-6A-67R engines. In 1993 the first three examples (FAC 1681, 1686 and 1656) were taken to the US for conversion and on October 17, 1994 FAC 1681 and 1656 were officially delivered to the Colombian Air Force. The aircraft also received a FLIR Systems Star Safire imaging turret under the nose, an Omega navigation system, new internal communications gear and comms equipment enabling contact with ground troops and the command post. All this was managed from a position in the front of the cargo cabin. The crew comprised two pilots, one navigator and systems operator (operating the FLIR/comms), one mechanic, one chief armourer and three other armourers (later reduced to two).

BELOW **The gunship based on Basler's BT-67 conversion has a longer fuselage, better to house the extra equipment** ALL SANTIAGO RIVAS

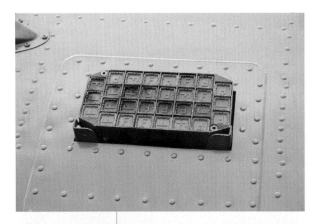

TOP LEFT **A Chaff and flare dispenser fitted to a Fantasma gunship**

ABOVE **Navigator position, with a large FLIR screen, communications equipment for contacting ground troops, the C3I2 control center and other aircraft**

The airframe FAC 1686 followed later, as did '1683 on February 12, 1996, FAC 165 on June 30, 1998, FAC 1659 and '1670 by June 30, 2000, FAC 1658 on January 31, 2001 and finally FAC 1667 shortly after. This last example was modified to replace FAC 1659, lost in an accident on September 2, 2000. Tragically, 1656 was also lost in an accident in 2002 when returning from a mission over Montezuma Hill, north of Pereira town.

The new gunships were designated AC-47T by the FAC and, as the FLIR increased the capabilities to operate at night, Capt Jorge Salazar, one of the first pilots of this model, used the callsign Fantasma (Phantom), as they could not be seen by the guerrillas and made little noise. This led to the type in general being branded Fantasma by the FAC.

Originally, the aircraft entered service with Escuadrón de Combate Táctico 113 Fantasma of the Comando Aéreo de Combate 1 (CACOM-1) at Base Aérea Germán Olano, in the town of Palanquero, Cundinamarca Department. However, they later served with the following units:

- **Escuadrón de Combate Táctico 213** of CACOM-2 at Base Aérea Capitán Luis Gómez Nino, Apiay, Meta

- **Escuadrón de Combate Táctico 313** of CACOM-3 at Base Aérea Mayor General Alberto Powels, Malambo, Barranquilla

- **Escuadrón de Combate Táctico 613** of CACOM-6 at Base Aérea Capitán Ernesto Esguerra Cubides, Tres Esquinas

- **Escuadrilla de Combate 1113** of Grupo Aéreo de Oriente, Marandúa, Vichada

- **Escuadrón de Combate 713** of the Escuela Militar de Aviación in Cali

Currently, they only operate from Palanquero, Apiay and Tres Esquinas, but they do temporarily deploy to the other bases.

Despite the M3 guns being accurate, their low rate of fire and problems with the barrels (which quickly became very hot) led to their replacement by two three-barrelled GAU-19 miniguns and a single .50 calibre.

Night vision goggles (NVGs) were supplied to the crews in 1997, which demanded modification of the cockpit lighting and use of special flares, LUU-19B/Bs, which could only be seen with NVGs.

Capt Juan Monsalve, former commander of ECT 213, explains: "the LUU-2A/B is mainly used for dissuasion, when there's information of a possible attack, the plane goes and drops a flare, so the guerrilla knows we are there and they have lost the [element of] surprise". The flares use a barometric system, and can be adjusted to turn on from between 250 to 10,000ft. Monsalve added: "When we support an air assault, we have to calculate the flare falls to the floor still burning, so the helicopter pilots can see the flare until it reaches the ground, because there couldn't be an element falling unseen in the middle of a lot of helicopters landing. I always try to put the flare as close as possible to the landing site, but not over them. We find the landing place; we must know the elevation, my height, the winds and how long they last burning, because the infra-red have a different duration to the others. One falls at 900ft per minute and the other at 700. We try to drop them in a way that they fall to one side or behind the helicopter pilots, so they are not blinded by their light. The chief armorer is the one in charge to drop them from the door, which is always open."

Another improvement is chaff and flare dispensers; while no aircraft has been shot down by guerrillas using missiles, the FAC learned they have obtained man-portable air defence systems and fired at a helicopter at least once, despite the weapon failing. Consequently, crews review the procedures to avoid anti-aircraft artillery and missiles in all briefings. Missile detection must be visual, as one crew member explained: "When we are over the targets, we are all looking outside and if someone sees a missile he must shout 'missile' and the position from where it comes. I reduce power to the minimum, drop the flares and turn to where the missile is coming [from]. Flares could be fired by the pilot, the navigator or from where the armourers are."

TOP LEFT **Cargo cabin, with the ammunition boxes on the right, the minigun at the back (in this case the aircraft has just one, but usually they carry two) and illumination flares on the left, which are dropped through the main door**

ABOVE **This pistol is used to fire small flares when operating over a location that could be attacked by guerrillas, to advertise that the gunship is present, and they have lost the surprise factor**

In the mid-2000s the Fantasma received a new navigation suite, with a higher definition FLIR Systems Brite Star II turret, satellite communications, GPS and other improvements. Also, a GIAT M-621 20mm gun was added to the mix, replacing one of the two GAU-19s usually installed. But the GIAT is only used when they have to operate against fortified targets or buildings, as it is not suitable against infantry – and the recoil can cause structural problems for the airframe. In 2017, one of the gunships was tested with a 30mm DEFA 552 gun from a retired Mirage 5COAM fighter aircraft – but wasn't fielded operationally.

Unfortunately, at 0745hrs on February 18, 2009 Fantasma FAC 1670 was lost in an accident while performing a training mission from the base of CACOM-1, killing the five occupants. The aircraft had a structural failure and began to plummet, with the wings collapsing before the fuselage hit the ground.

The main Fantasma unit is Escuadrón de Combate Táctico 113 at Germán Olano Air Base in Palanquero, about 62 miles northwest of Bogotá, where three of the six operational aircraft are based (there usually are five 'good to go' and one under maintenance).

Major Miguel Ángel Cubides from this squadron has six years flying the gunship and explains: "In the past the Fantasma was used in a very offensive way… the troops were attacked and the Fantasma arrived, the troops were contacted, we found from where the attack was coming and force was applied, responding to the attack. With the mutation of the terrorist organisations, that mission has been a little neglected, but we still support the troops. Now the guerrillas do not capture towns or outposts as in the past. The intensity has decreased, but whenever there is an attack against the public force or the population, the plane arrives, and they calm down immediately. At that moment it is a very dissuasive weapon, which has the ability to search, detect and attack, and they know that they do not have the capacity to do anything to us and that we have the capacity to do them a lot of damage. So, they fall back."

A typical mission, Cubides explains, starts when they are informed of an attack and: "…in 20 minutes we are in the air, we run to the plane, we do the checks, take off and we proceed to the target. Once in the area we make contact with the troops and they tell us where the attack is coming from or from where it is presumed, by intelligence information, that they are going to attack them. We do the search and if there is an active threat, we will neutralise it, and if there is no active threat, we will verify the area where they were attacked and the surroundings to provide security. If required, we launch an illumination flare, to give confidence to the troops and let the enemy know that we are over them. Sometimes we are two or three hours over the target, depending on the situation. We give security to the troops and let them reposition themselves if they are attacked, so that the enemy does not attack them again in the same place, and they take more advantageous positions."

Combined operations

Escuadrón 213 at Apiay, has one of the other Fantasmas currently in service, together with one attack Black Hawk (called Arpía), one combat search and rescue Black Hawk (called Ángel) and three Cessna Grand Caravans (one for medevac, one for intelligence and the other for transport). Monsalve explains how they operate: "It all starts when the ground troops are in combat and they send the request to the brigade that makes contact with

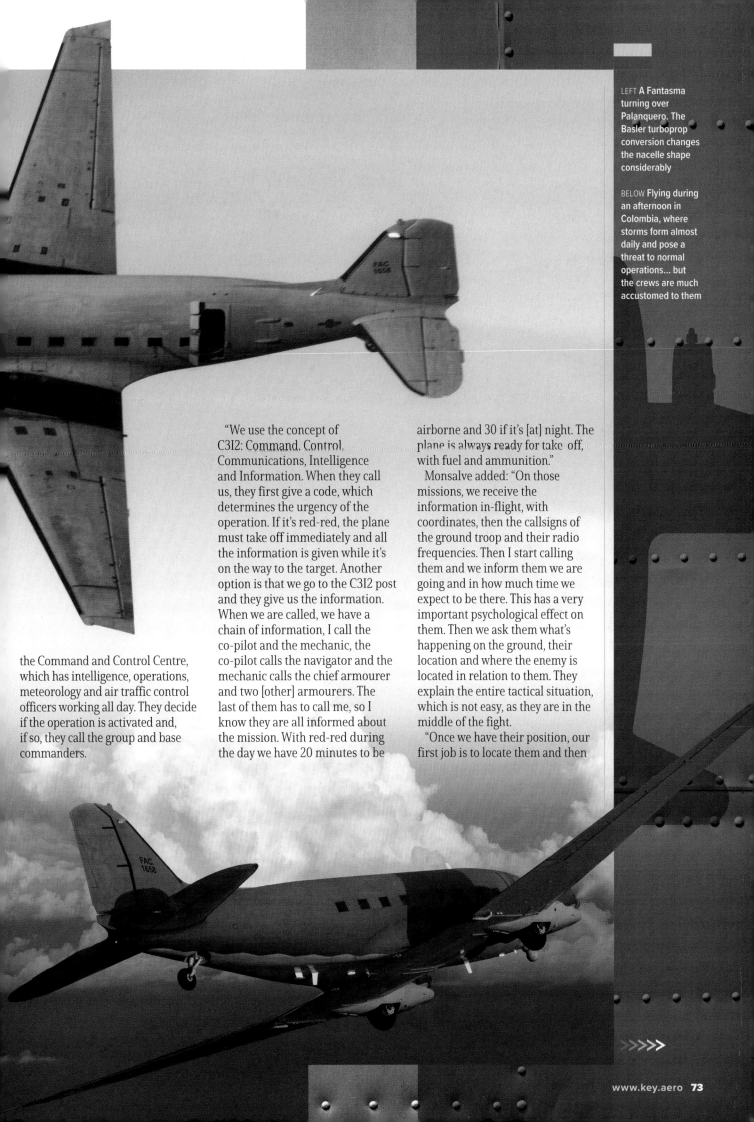

"We use the concept of C3I2: Command, Control, Communications, Intelligence and Information. When they call us, they first give a code, which determines the urgency of the operation. If it's red-red, the plane must take off immediately and all the information is given while it's on the way to the target. Another option is that we go to the C3I2 post and they give us the information. When we are called, we have a chain of information, I call the co-pilot and the mechanic, the co-pilot calls the navigator and the mechanic calls the chief armourer and two [other] armourers. The last of them has to call me, so I know they are all informed about the mission. With red-red during the day we have 20 minutes to be

the Command and Control Centre, which has intelligence, operations, meteorology and air traffic control officers working all day. They decide if the operation is activated and, if so, they call the group and base commanders.

airborne and 30 if it's [at] night. The plane is always ready for take off, with fuel and ammunition."

Monsalve added: "On those missions, we receive the information in-flight, with coordinates, then the callsigns of the ground troop and their radio frequencies. Then I start calling them and we inform them we are going and in how much time we expect to be there. This has a very important psychological effect on them. Then we ask them what's happening on the ground, their location and where the enemy is located in relation to them. They explain the entire tactical situation, which is not easy, as they are in the middle of the fight.

"Once we have their position, our first job is to locate them and then

>>>>>

FAC Douglas AC-47 and Basler AC-47T Fantasma

Serial	Code number	Delivered after conversion	Notes
1650	14056/25501	Not converted	Built as C-47A-30-DK. Former USAF 43-48240 and FAC 650. Lost in accident Aug 30, 1988
1652		Not converted	Former FAC 652. Not converted into BT-67 and retired from service early 1990s
1654	14847/26292	12-2-96	Built as C-47B-10-DK. Former USAF 43-49031 and FAC 654A. Basler conversion kit 26. In service
1656		17-10-94	Lost in accident 2002 at Cerro Montezuma
1658	15793/32541	31-1-01	Built as C-47B-25-DK. Former USAF 44-76209. Converted to Dakota IV for RAF as KN292. Delivered to Armée de l'Air as 476209. To French Navy as 76709. Basler conversion kit 37. In service
1659	16236/32984	30-6-98	Built as C-47B-30-DK. Former USAF 44-76652. Basler conversion kit 29. Lost in accident Sept 2, 2000
1667	19052	2002	Built as C-47A-65-DL. Former USAF 42-100589. Basler conversion kit 38. In service
1670	19125	30-6-00	Built as C-47A-70-DL. Former USAF 42-100662. Basler conversion kit 36. Former N40359. Lost in accident Feb 18, 2009 during training flight
1681	16500/33248	17-10-94	Built as C-47B-35-DK. Former USAF 44-76916. Converted to Dakota IV for RAF as KN605. To Royal Netherlands AF as ZU-12 and X-12. Former FAC 681. Basler conversion kit 23. In service. Wears '20 years of the Fantasma' markings
1683	15692/27137	unknown	Built as C-47B-20-DK. Former USAF 43-49876. Armée de l'Air as 349876 and Israeli AF as 4X-FNQ. Former N472DK. In service
1686	13998/25443	1994	Built as Douglas R4D-5 for USN, Bu.No. 17245. Converted to C-47A-30-DK. Former USAF 43-48182. To N1561M and later to N54V at Piedmont Air Lines, named 'Sand Hills Pacemaker'. In service

they guide us to the enemy, they give us a distance and a direction, and we start the search. Once we find the enemy, we start the attack."

Currently, almost all operations are during the night and the navigator uses the FLIR to locate both the enemy and friendly troops. In the past, the guerrillas used to keep fighting when the Fantasmas arrived, but this meant they were easier to find by the pilot, who saw their weapons fire. Now, they have learned to stop firing and try to hide and separate from each other, making them more difficult to be chased. As they are usually armed with small weapons, and the Fantasma attacks from an altitude of 4,000ft, they don't fire on the aircraft, as they are out of range.

The gunship also acts as forward air control and command post; the navigator controls the operation of the aircraft and is in permanent contact with the ground units. He also coordinates the attacks of other aircraft, according to the position of the ground troops. They usually operate together with the attack squadrons, equipped with Embraer Super Tucanos and Cessna A-37B Dragonfly, as well as the Sikorsky AH-60L Arpía III attack helicopters. Usually, Fantasmas have up to ten hours' endurance.

As the machine guns are fixed, the precision depends on the proficiency of the pilot, who aims with the whole aircraft. "Wind, speed, height and banking all affect it", explains Monsalve and adds that the best is to keep the same speed, altitude and bank angle, but over the mountains it's often not possible. "With every burst you adjust the aiming. When I fly, I see the sight, the ground, and my screen to check what the navigator is watching on the FLIR. The key is to work well between the navigator and the pilot. If you have a good navigator it's super, as he must have the capacity to identify the guerrillas; they hide in the trees, walk like animals, they have tactics. The FLIR has a laser and I only have to aim to where the laser is. The navigator gives me the azimuth and I look that way. In daylight it's more difficult, I can't see the laser and it's [harder] to see the light of the sight," adds Monsalve.

Other missions
One of the main missions of the Fantasma is also to act as command post, not just on attack operations, but also to support medical evacuations. In those cases, they keep flying over the site from

where the evacuation will take place and when the helicopter or aircraft arrives (usually a Huey 2, Black Hawk or Grand Caravan), they drop a flare to illuminate the area and keep orbiting until the evacuation is completed.

Since 2010 the problem of illegal mining, in most cases performed by guerrillas, has burgeoned and the government decided to create a special police unit for ground interdiction, supported by the army and air force. The Fantasma is used as a command post during operations against those mines.

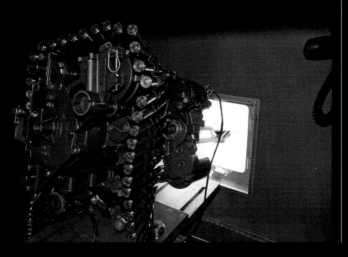

LEFT A GAU-19 .50 cal Minigun on a Fantasma.

BELOW Evident here are Minigun and GIAT guns, and ports above the door for firing the flare pistol. Notice the airstream deflectors along the immediate left of the door.

As there are often many civilians involved, they can't make an air strike, but the aircraft are always armed in case there's an attack by guerrillas or they are defending the location.

They look for ground troops with the FLIR and if there are more mines in the area they guide the police forces to them so they can destroy the machinery. The main advantage of the Fantasma is its very long endurance, as those operations are usually very drawn-out affairs. Monsalve recalls that they had an operation which lasted 7 hrs 20mins, in which they found

more mines and machinery and had to summon the police.

Another operation is against drug trafficking on the Caribbean Sea. In the past, drugs were transported via the Pacific Ocean to the south of the country, but currently, many drugs are taken to Venezuela and from there to the USA via the Caribbean, through Central America or one of the islands en route. Since 2013 the FAC has operated an aircraft from San Andrés Island for the 'Astim' Operations, against illegal maritime traffic. The Fantasma works with a Cessna SR26 Horus,

which is a Citation with an APG-66 radar. Horus enables the detection of the faster vessels used by drug traffickers and then the Fantasma is sent to follow them. The gunship's relatively slow speed and endurance is perfect for following criminal watercraft and guiding the ships of the Colombian Navy or US Coast Guard to capture them. They fly at about 7 miles behind, on an S-pattern, and produce very   good results.

Despite the age of the Fantasmas, they continue to be extremely useful and will undoubtedly soldier on for many years to come. ●

ABOVE LEFT Fantasma FAC 1658 airborne. Its Minigun is clearly visible, as is the air intake replacing one of the windows, used to create an air stream to the back door, thus allowing gun fumes to escape

BELOW LEFT Two of the Fantasmas based at Palanquero, one being about to depart on a night mission

Quelling
THE REBELS

During the 1970s, C-47s played an important role in the Rhodesian Bush War as **Andrew Thomas** recounts

Douglas's C-47 was the main transport aircraft for most air arms during the years following World War Two. Few, however, had such a long operational longevity as those used by the Rhodesian Air Force which, as well as a general transport, also used them in action for high- and low-level parachuting, electronic/signals reconnaissance and as an airborne command post.

The first military Dakota in Rhodesia (now Zimbabwe) was a single aircraft gifted by the South African premier, Field Marshal Jan Christian Smuts, in November 1947. Given the serial SR25 it became part of the small Communications Flight of the permanent Southern Rhodesia Staff Corps based at Cranborne, near the capital Salisbury (now Harare) under Lt Harold Hawkins. Soon afterwards it became part of the reconstituted Southern Rhodesian Air Force and in 1953 was incorporated into 3 Squadron SRAF when it formed at the new base of New Sarum, south of Salisbury.

Vampire ferry
The first major task for the new squadron came on September 12, 1953 when Maj Harold Hawkins flew the Dakota to the UK to support the ferrying of de Havilland Vampires from the UK to Rhodesia, with the first jets arriving on December 12, 1953. The transport positioned spares and servicing personnel along the route, and this was repeated during further ferry flights in 1954 and '55. As part of the expansion of the SRAF, seven Dakotas were received as a gift from the British Government, serialled SR151-SR157. The Federation of Rhodesia and Nyasaland was formed on August 1, 1953 when defence became a federal responsibility so on October 15, 1954 the SRAF became the Royal Rhodesian AF, and its aircraft serials were then prefixed RRAF. The Dakotas were used for routine work throughout the federation but in January 1956, by which time Sqn Ldr Ted Cunnison was CO, the Squadron's Dakotas undertook photo recce and survey work, including for the construction of the Kariba Dam, for which an aircraft was modified to carry a Williamson Mk.1 survey camera.

The RRAF was also committed to the wider defence of the Middle East alongside the RAF. Thus, in early January 1958 five Dakotas flew personnel and equipment of a detachment of 1 Squadron Vampires for aerial policing operations in Aden; this became a regular event. Closer to home in late February 1959, due to unrest in Nyasaland, reinforcements were sent with the Dakotas airlifting 129 troops to Blantyre on the 20th alone. The State of Emergency declared on March 3 resulted in a hectic period for the squadron with more than 1,000 troops being flown in over a three-day period. Later in the year a new task was given to the Dakotas, when the Parachute Evaluation Detachment (PED) formed and 3 Squadron assumed a new role, namely parachute dropping, which later came to the fore during the long years of the Bush War. The first live drop during the evaluation period took place in February 1960 and in August 1962 the PED became C Squadron (Rhodesian) Special Air Service, so starting a long and successful association between the units.

In early July 1960, the squadron was involved in the crisis in Katanga Province of the former Belgian Congo, flying by day and night ferrying people from Katanga

to N'dola in Northern Rhodesia – and transporting rations and bedding on return trips. The following year when the Viscount airliners of Central African Airways were grounded between January and March, RRAF Dakotas flew 19 replacement services. In June 1963, the squadron supported the detachment of RRAF Canberras to work with the RAF in Cyprus and later airdropped relief supplies to isolated communities during the disastrous flooding in Kenya during 1962-63.

However, the 'winds of change' were blowing and on December 31, 1963 the federation was dissolved pending the independence of Northern Rhodesia as Zambia, and Nyasaland as Malawi. Thus, among other equipment, four Dakotas (RRAF152, '154, '156 and '157), were transferred to the Northern Rhodesia Air Wing, which soon became the Zambian Air Force.

Rain makers

While then under the leadership of Sqn Ldr W H Smith on February 7, 1964, four replacement aircraft were bought from the SAAF. The existing machines were re-numbered as 3 Squadron

returned to a strength of eight, serialled RRAF702 to 709. The first signs of African nationalist unrest in Rhodesia were becoming evident when, on July 4, the first terror-inspired murder of a white farmer occurred. The political situation worsened as the Rhodesian Government resisted moves to majority rule and resulted in the Unilateral Declaration of Independence (UDI) from Britain on November 11, 1965. The RRAF was cut off from its close links with the RAF overnight and acted as a catalyst for further terror activity by Nationalist groups, notably the Zimbabwe African People's Union and the Marxist Zambian African National Union with their respective armed wings, the Zimbabwe People's Revolutionary Army (ZIPRA) and Zimbabwe African National Liberation Army (ZANLA).

Transport operations continued as normal for 3 Squadron, though in May 1967, when commanded by Sqn Ldr Peter Barnett, it participated in a rain-making project with the University of Rhodesia and the Meteorological Office. Dakota R7307 was fitted with two burners, in which silver iodide and acetone were pumped, mixed and ignited. The resulting microscopic smoke particles were vented into the clouds, so promoting rainfall. So-called 'cloud seeding' continued each summer until the aircraft was written off

TOP **A 3 Squadron Dakota is serviced at Blantyre, Nyasaland in June 1959 at the time of disturbances in the country** RRAF

ABOVE **Rhodesian AF pilot wings.**

LEFT **As the war progressed through the mid-1970s, dropping troops by parachute – often from low level – assumed increasing importance during 'Fireforce' and cross-border operations** RHOD AF

BELOW **These smart 3 Squadron Dakotas at New Sarum in 1965 display the single assegai roundel adopted by the RRAF from 1964** RRAF

in an accident at Rushinga airfield on February 21, 1975. It had been named *Chaminuka* after the local African rain god.

Just after Christmas 1967, Operation Cauldron was launched by the Rhodesian Security Forces, in response to an incursion by ZIPRA insurgents – resulting in a huge increase in workload – typically with 150,000lb of freight a month being lifted. The pace gradually increased as the Bush War intensified, and from 1968, 3 Squadron was used to resupply forward airfields and to move troops to forward areas.

(Psy Ops) specialists and varied according to the message to be conveyed. Command of the unit was assumed by Sqn Ldr M K Gedye that September. When the crew of a Canberra ejected over the Wankie Game Reserve (now Hwange National park) on October 28, 1969 a Dakota was scrambled to search for them and the crew successfully co-ordinated the rescue.

Sky-shouting from a Dakota was used to good effect in early 1970 during Operation Teak around Victoria Falls and Birch, resulting in several terrorists

conducted eight days of 'sky-shout' operations around Mueda in northern Mozambique, in support of Portuguese forces. This was repeated the following month and on November 29, Dakotas supported Operation Apollo against ZANLA and FRELIMO in Tete Province of Mozambique, southwest of the Cabora Bassa Gorge (now Cahora Bassa) and this continued as Operation Jacaranda into 1971. Meanwhile, in Rhodesia the rainmaking project also continued besides more routine tasks.

'Special' parachuting

During September and October

One innovation trialled with the Dakotas beginning in February 1968 was 'sky-shouting', similar to those sorties conducted by the RAF during the Malayan Emergency. Two large loudspeakers were fitted in the doorway of the Dakota, from which recorded voice messages were broadcast. Sky-shouting was carried out in areas where it was known that terrorists were operating and was often combined with leaflet dropping. The aircraft was flown in a gentle turn to port over the intended area, at a height of 1,500 to 2000ft above ground level. The tapes were produced by Psychological Operations

surrendering. Some commented they had become so demoralised with being on the run (from the Rhodesians) that they heard the broadcast message inviting them to surrender with great relief. That was the final operation for the Royal Rhodesian Air Force, as on March 2 Rhodesia was declared a republic, thus the markings were changed to reflect this.

Freedom fighters of the Mozambique Liberation Front (FRELIMO) were also active in the neighbouring Portuguese colony of Mozambique and during July a 3 Squadron Dakota

in great secrecy at sunset on January 19, Flt Lt Ivan Holshausen, flying Dakota R7303, dropped two four-man SAS pathfinder teams from 11,000ft on the first airborne military operation outside Rhodesia. The main drop was conducted later that night and the men were resupplied by Dakota for the next month. Later, a journalist accompanied a supply sortie to the SAS force at Macombe, reporting: "The aircraft closed in on the kopjes [small rocky hills] of the escarpment and suddenly plunged into a blinding cloudbank. It was frightening

1971, the squadron supported intensive free-fall parachute training with the SAS, including night descents. The aircraft could carry up to 20 paratroopers in this role, though 16 was more usual. In addition to training, on September 15 Dakota R7303, flown by Flt Lt Peter Bater, dropped an SAS team into Lake Kariba during Operation Lobster. More of the squadron's activities then focused on supporting Security Force operations such as on December 30, when Flt Lt Alan Bradnick transported SAS troops to Musengezi, in Dakota R7308.

In March 1972 Sqn Ldr George Alexander took command and he was to see the unit through most of its operations over the next six years. The first major task, however, was to fly rescue teams to Wankie in early June after a mine explosion killed 460 miners.

Increasing enemy activity at the start of 1973 prompted the beginning of Operation Hurricane in northeast Rhodesia, as the conflict entered its second, and ultimately bloody, phase. Initial bad weather made road movement difficult, so the army was dependent on 3 Squadron to move men, fuel and rations. Night supply drops were also conducted, and casualties evacuated, sometimes from primitive bush strips illuminated solely by vehicle headlights. Then

for a while, the tops of some of the kopjes were actually above us as we wove our way through. The supplies would be dropped from about 300ft. The green light flashed and two 'shooks' went lurching out, their 'chutes billowing open and they hit dead on target."

'Fireforce'

During 1973 the Fireforce concept began to develop where a group of about 60 troops with helicopters – and usually a Dakota – were held

>>>>

ABOVE **Troops of the Rhodesian African Rifles board a Dakota on a forward strip before moving to their next location** RHOD AF

ABOVE RIGHT **C-47B RRAF152 of 3 Squadron embarking passengers on a routine flight in mid-1950** K SMY

BELOW **Wearing the then new Rhodesian AF roundel, Dakota R7307 lifts off from New Sarum on a routine transport schedule** D BECKER

at very high readiness at a Forward Air Field (FAF) under direct control of the local Joint Operations Centre. When an insurgent group was detected, the Fireforce would move with the assault group being flown in by helicopter, often with a blocking force dropped beyond by Dakota, towards which the insurgents would be driven. The concept gradually evolved and proved highly effective.

Dakota numbers in 3 Squadron also gradually increased, with two acquired from South Africa in March 1973 as R3711 and R7312, while a year later two more were obtained from Central African Airways, being serialled R7313 and R7134, the latter kept in VIP configuration and used extensively to fly the President, Prime Minister Ian Smith and other VIPs around the country. The Rhodesians' position was weakened at this time when a coup in Portugal brought about an immediate withdrawal from its African colonies, so presenting another hostile state and a lengthy border to police.

An aircraft was lost on February 21, 1975 when Dakota R7307 flown

by Flt Lt Ed Paintin ground looped on landing at FAF9 Rutenga and was wrecked, fortunately without any serious injuries. There were further sky-shout flights during March in the Angwa River area by a Dakota flown by Fg Off Noel van Hoff. The development of new high-altitude low-opening (known as HALO) parachuting techniques from the Dakota also continued with the Parachute School. The highlight of the period, however, was on April 7 when AVM Harold Hawkins presented 3 Squadron with its Standard. After this brief diversion it was back to operations such as that on June 23, when four Dakotas participated in a large Fireforce sweep operation, but with disappointing results. A short while later the CO was interviewed for the *Illustrated Life of Rhodesia* and described his squadron's aircraft: "The Dakota is the grand old lady of the Rhodesian Air Force – sturdy, trustworthy, capable of nipping in and out of short dirt strips even with a sizeable load on board. There'll never be another aircraft built like this one."

The operational tempo was unrelenting and by then all external markings had been removed from RhodAF aircraft, though the Dakotas retained their silver and white colours. A typical operation came mid-morning on September 30, 1976 when a Fireforce was called out from FAF9 Rutenga. The Dakota dropped three sticks of SAS troopers to form a stop line and later flew fuel into a strip and lifted out a troop of the Rhodesian Army's special forces unit, the Selous Scouts. Twenty-eight insurgents were killed in the successful two-day operation.

However, the decision of the SAAF to recall most of its helicopters that had been operating in Rhodesia resulted in a greatly increased workload for 3 Squadron Dakotas, including more operational parachuting. The threat from ground fire also increased and on October 7 a Dakota was hit during an operational drop, but the damage was slight.

Developing roles
From 1977, external attacks on ZIPRA and ZANLA training camps in neighbouring countries were

"...with the emerging threats most of the squadron's aircraft were camouflaged and fitted with an anti SA-7 missile shield over the exhausts"

considered to reduce incursions into Rhodesia. These large-scale external raids resulted in new roles for 3 Squadron's 'Daks'. To try to identify the location of enemy encampments, or to provide real-time information during an operation, a Dakota was modified as an electronic intelligence collector. This aircraft collected and analysed electronic communications as well as missile and surveillance radar data. Intelligence-gathering flights were of high strategic value given the remote nature of insurgent bases. With various 'lumps and bumps', and sprouting numerous aerials, it soon became known as the 'Warthog'. Later, another Dakota was configured as an airborne command post, the 'command Dak'. Also at about this time, despite UN sanctions, three more Dakotas, R3700, R3701 and R7310 were received from various sources and with the emerging threats most of the squadron's aircraft were camouflaged and fitted with an anti SA-7 missile shield over the exhausts.

However, 1977 started badly when, on January 6 during a resupply operation in the low veld at very low altitude, R7034 hit overhead cables – killing pilots Sqn Ldr Peter Barnett and Flt Lt Dave Mallett, plus army despatcher Cpl Bradley, though three others survived uninjured.

Four days after this tragedy, as a precursor to a major air attack on a ZANLA group on the Madulo Pan in Mozambique, a Dakota dropped two Selous Scouts to set up a marker beacon on the target that was attacked by Canberras the following night.

Another notable operation was when Dakotas provided airdrop support to a boat-mounted SAS operation attacking FRELIMO positions along the shores of the Cahora Bassa Lake. When in late May a large quantity of enemy arms and equipment was discovered by the Selous Scouts across the border in Mozambique, near Mapai, Operation Aztec was launched by Dakota to recover this valuable horde. After two successful flights, R3702 flown by Flt Lt Jerry Lynch was taking off at dusk with the aid of truck lights. Just as it became airborne the aircraft was hit by machine gun fire and an RPG-7 rocket, which killed co-pilot Flt Lt Bruce Collocott instantly. Lynch successfully stopped the aircraft and the surviving crew evacuated as it caught fire and burned out. It was another heavy blow.

>>>>>

ABOVE **On one of the last operations, this Dakota is flying a supply drop to the SAS on Mozambique's Gorongoza plateau, on October 9, 1979** VIA GP CAPT B SYKES

BELOW **A Dakota on the airfield at Gatooma in September 1979, shortly before the ceasefire** VIA GP CAPT B SYKES

Further on in that year, in late October, Flt Lt Lynch's crew dropped troops at night from R3708 to interdict a convoy moving the FRELIMO 4th Brigade from Maputo to Mapai. After the drop the Dakota conducted bombing using small 'Alpha' anti-personnel bombs to create a diversion… but was heavily engaged by ground fire and the aircraft sustained several hits. The crew flew a resupply drop the next night. During another nocturnal supply drop in northern Mozambique, by Flt Lt Wally Galloway's crew in early November, the despatchers rigged a machine gun in the para door and when the aircraft came under fire, returned the compliment!

Cross-border attacks

Within days came the huge Rhodesian raids on the ZANLA HQ camp at Chimoio and at Tembue in Mozambique, which hit both targets successfully. The Dakotas dropped paras for both parts of Operation Dingo that commander operations Lt Gen Peter Walls co-ordinated from the 'Command Dak', specially fitted with additional air-to-ground communications. At dawn on November 23, six Dakotas led by Flt Lt Bob d'Hotman carried almost 150 paratroopers, which were dropped to seal off Chimoia before the arrival of a Canberra and Hunter attack, and the main force by helicopter. After recovering to base the Rhodesians then headed for Tembue, which was a more complex operation with a very similar profile and that too was successful.

The increasingly violent Bush War took a savage new turn when on September 3, 1978 a civilian Air Rhodesia Vickers Viscount was shot down near Kariba with an SA-7 missile fired by a ZIPRA unit. The guerrillas then massacred the survivors they found. Another major assault was mounted against the ZANLA complex at Chimoio on September 20, before one of the most famous incidents of the war that became known as the 'Green Leader' attack. Operation Gatling was a raid on October 19 against the ZIPRA camp at Westlands Farm, just ten miles from the Zambian capital of Lusaka, which housed around 4,000 guerrillas and was a direct response to the airliner incident. The assault opened with an air attack followed by a large para and heliborne operation, all controlled from the Command Dak by Air Cdre Norman Walsh along with Lt Gen Walls. The Rhodesians also radioed Lusaka airport: "You are to keep your air traffic on the ground for another ten minutes." A civilian aircraft then asked who had priority, receiving the reply from the tower: "I think the Rhodesians do!" On the next phase six more Dakotas flew at low level to drop SAS men on a complex at Mkushi, which was cleared the next day after mopping up. Then shortly

LEFT CENTRE **On May 30, 1977 Dakota R3702 was struck by ground fire while taking off from Mapai in Mozambique, and was completely destroyed** VIA GP CAPT B SYKES

LEFT **Men of the Selous Scouts prepare for a training jump from a 3 Squadron Dakota in 1978** VIA WG CDR P COOKE

LEFT **A trio of Dakotas out on a para-drop operation, probably into Mozambique during the last year of the war** AIR MARSHAL N WALSH

BELOW LEFT **When landing at Mabalauta in southeast Rhodesia after a resupply drop in Mozambique, the wingtip of this Dakota struck a tree while evading an SA-7 missile, requiring emergency repairs** VIA WG CDR P COOKE

26th a joint attack by Rhodesian and SAAF Canberras was mounted against the ZIPRA training camp at Luso, deep in central Angola. Once again, the operation was co-ordinated by the Command Dak and two others provided search and rescue cover. The violence of

before Christmas came Operation Vodka, a raid into a Zambian ZIPRA camp to rescue prisoners. It began with Dakotas dropping 21 men of the Selous Scouts, which one of the crew described as: "...looking villainous in an assortment of stained and dirty clothing, carrying AK-47 rifles like the guerrillas." The whole operation was coordinated from the Command Dak, informed by operators in the Warthog.

Climax

After a second airliner was shot down on February 11, 1979, on the

RIGHT **By 1981, Dakota 7310 had been stripped of camouflage for VIP use by the Air Force of Zimbabwe** AFZ

ABOVE **The shattered remains of Dakota R7034 after it crashed during operations at the Lundi River near Chirezdi, on January 6, 1977** AVM I HARVEY

BELOW **To support a 'Fireforce' package, a Dakota was usually positioned alongside the troops and helicopters at a forward strip, ready to conduct an immediate parachute response** J BOYD

the Bush War continued to increase as it reached its bloody climax with increasing cross border raids, in which 3 Squadron Dakotas played a full part either dropping paras or in the command and control role. One was a daring mission on the ZIPRA leader's home in Lusaka on June 26, when the signals intelligence-equipped Dakota proved particularly useful. On one occasion the Warthog was tracked down the Zambezi Valley by two Zambian MiG fighters, but escaped by low flying.

Terror incidents proliferated across Rhodesia and on September 5 came Operation Uric, a major endeavour involving most of the Rhod AF, including 12 Dakotas. The raid was against a huge enemy camp at Barragem in Mozambique, which was heavily defended, as was the co-incident attack against Mapai; ZANLA incurred heavy losses but so, on this occasion, did the Rhodesians.

Operation Miracle against the ZANLA complex at Chimoio began on September 26, with 3 Squadron Dakotas again heavily involved, but again the target was heavily defended. The month also brought a return to sky-shout operations when a Dakota flew over a contact area carrying captured terrorists, who urged their comrades in the bush to surrender.

Within days a raid was mounted on the Chambesi rail bridge in northeast Zambia, in which a Dakota dropped a free-fall SAS team to recce the target before others were inserted to blow up

the bridge, in one of the most successful operations of the war. Resupply operations to SAS patrols in the Gorongoza plateau of Mozambique continued, while on October 18, during an operation against ZIPRA on a large camp near the Kariba to Lusaka road, Dakotas dropped troops after an air strike and another circled the area firing flares to illuminate the area for the troops.

From November 16 during the last major operation outside Rhodesia, the Dakotas parachuted teams into Zambia and then conducted airborne resupply. Soon after, with the start of peace negotiations in London, external operations were halted and a ceasefire was declared on December 28.

After elections, Rhodesia became independent as Zimbabwe on April 18, 1980 and the Dakotas continued in use with the new Air Force of Zimbabwe, but from 1983 were gradually replaced and finally withdrawn in 1991. ●

Bohemian
HAULERS

The process of rebuilding and returning to some form of normality following World War Two was a difficult process in many countries. That was particularly true for those states in Europe that had been conquered in one form or another by Nazi Germany. The pre-war independent state of Czechoslovakia had ceased to exist during March 1939, having already been dismembered the previous September in the notorious Munich Agreement.

Prior to the take-over, five DC-2s were allocated Czechoslovak civil registrations, OK-AIA to OK-AID and OK-AIZ. In addition, four DC-3-220 also received 'OK' registrations, OK-AIE to OK-AIH. A principal operator was ČLS (Československá letecká společnost, literally the Czechoslovak Airline Company).

With the German takeover of Czechoslovakia in March 1939, three of the DC-2s and all four DC-3s were seized and allocated German civil registrations, the 'Threes' becoming D-AAIE to D-AAIH.

Skytrains arrive

At the end of the war the Czechoslovak capital, Prague, was liberated by the capital's own home army on May 8, 1945, while Soviet tanks waited to make a ceremonial arrival the following day.

Czechoslovakia was then soon reconstituted, and the country was reunited with an end to the former Nazi 'Protectorate' and the coming together of the Czech and Slovak parts. Initially, much of western Czechoslovakia was held by US forces, with a major Soviet presence in the east. During the following years it appeared that the country would be western-leaning, and to that end a considerable amount of aid, especially from the US, was forthcoming.

The Czechoslovak state airline, ČSA, had originally been founded during 1923, and was reconstituted after the war; ČSA originally stood for Československé státní aerolinie (Czechoslovak State Airlines), later shortened to Československé aerolinie. It immediately found itself lacking modern airliners.

The end of hostilities made thousands of USAAF C-47 Skytrains redundant virtually overnight. But in contrast to the many US fighters and bombers scrapped during the following years, the C-47 fleet largely survived, and many airframes ended up

Among the many post-war operators of the C-47, Czechoslovakia used the type in both civil and military roles. **Malcolm V Lowe** explains the Skytrain's little-known service in this Central European country

'de-mobbed' in civil colours. One of the countries that benefited from this sudden availability of relatively cheap transport aircraft was Czechoslovakia, and in the following decade or so the C-47 became a part of the country's post-war aviation revival. Deliveries began in 1946, the first recorded examples including C-47A 42-23602 on March 14, 1946, this airframe becoming OK-WDA with ČSA.

Many, but not all of the subsequent deliveries of Skytrains, were made to ČSA. Some passed to other organisations, including the famous footwear and fashion accessories manufacturer Bat'a. Three examples were registered to Bat'a, two during 1946. They were C-47A 42-23507/OK-WBC, and an early production C-47 41-18516/OK-WBA, which was the oldest

Skytrain to reach the Czechoslovak civil register. The third Bat'a example was C-47A 43-15072/OK-XBC, which was delivered during August 1946.

In total, Czechoslovak documents of the time identify 66 C-47/C-47A/C-47B that reached the country between March 1946 and September 1947. The final delivery appears to have been C-47A 42-32925 on September 17, 1947, which became O ČSA's K-XDN.

Due to their military origins, these aircraft all started out with very austere interiors. Although some work had been performed internally on several aircraft prior to delivery, they needed considerable work to 'civilianise' and make them comfortable enough for airline passengers and their crew members. Although ČSA attempted

to standardise the interiors across its fleet, there were variations, especially as some aircraft were put into service comparatively soon after their arrival in Czechoslovakia. Nevertheless, ČSA's own workshops did a good job on making the airframes as comfortable as possible, and they were among the better civilian conversions of former military C-47s. This work effectively turned the aircraft into DC-3 civil configuration, but with many differences compared to the original version of pre-war Douglas manufacture.

Military deliveries

Other Skytrains from among the 66 recorded arrivals were passed directly to Czechoslovakia's air force. This organisation had originally been formed following

ABOVE **Former USAAF C-47A 42-23523/ OK-WDZ of ČSA sits on the tarmac at Frankfurt in March 1953,** having been deliberately flown there by its pilot who defected, together with five other people onboard. Tragically, having returned to Czechoslovakia, the aircraft was destroyed in a fatal accident during January 1956 KEY COLLECTION

BELOW **On outside display in a new public area at the Letecké Muzeum, the DC-3-229 is painted in the dark khaki green over light blue colour scheme of the air force's D-47 fleet in the 1950s** MALCOLM V LOWE

RIGHT **A Czechoslovak-operated Lisunov Li-2 transport receives maintenance outside in the sunshine. The photograph was probably taken at Kbely airfield where the 1st Air Transport Regiment was based** VIA MALCOLM V LOWE

RIGHT CENTRE **A ČSA C-47 with its very smart flight crew. The type came to be popular in Czechoslovakia, where it was a workhorse on domestic and some international routes** MALCOLM V LOWE COLLECTION

RIGHT **Czechoslovak military C-47s were designated D-47, and carried out many of the functions of their former USAAF use. Here, Czechoslovak paratroops prepare to board the D-47 coded 'D-18'... former USAAF C-47B 43-48406, later coded '8406'** MALCOLM V LOWE COLLECTION

Lisunov Li-2 in Czechoslovakia

Following the communist take-over of Czechoslovakia during 1948, an increasing number of Soviet aircraft types were exported to the country for Czechoslovak military service. Included was the Li-2, this type serving as a transport alongside the Skytrain and helping to replace the ageing Junkers Ju 52/3m (D-7). So far 19 Li-2 airframes have been positively identified in Czechoslovak service, these operating with the 1st Air Transport Regiment and specialist units. The final Li-2 example was withdrawn from use during 1967. A preserved Li-2 is currently displayed in the Letecké Muzeum at Kbely.

the creation of the country, one of its several titles being the Československé vojenské letectvo. Reconstituted in Czechoslovakia following the end of World War Two, the air force designated the C-47 as the D-47 ('D' standing for dopravní or transport).

According to records held by the Military History Institute in Prague detailing the arrivals and serial numbers, at least 19 C-47A/Bs were received for military service, or served for part of their lives with the air force. Initially coded rather confusingly on their fuselage sides in a 'D' numerical sequence, later some reverted to the 'last four' of their former USAAF serial numbers. These airframes were, eventually, mainly allocated to the 1. ldp (1. letecký dopravní pluk – 1st Air Transport Regiment) later redesignated as the 1. dlp (1. dopravní letecký pluk, with the same translation). This unit was based at Kbely airfield on the outskirts of Prague, an air base with long-standing connections to Czechoslovak transport aviation.

The exact total of C-47 airframes eventually fielded by the Czechoslovak military is complicated by the fact that some

ČSA examples were temporarily used by the air force as required. On the other hand, some of the D-47 fleet were contracted to ČSA when needed.

Changed direction

The communist seizure of power in Czechoslovakia during February 1948 had a profound influence on the country's relations with the West. Deliveries of many types of goods, including aircraft, rapidly dried up from the US and its allies. Instead, a stream of often poorer quality material started to come from the direction of the Soviet Union.

One of the better products that reached Czechoslovakia in the following years was the Lisunov

Li-2, the Soviet licence-built interpretation of the DC-3/C-47 (see pages 46-49). In the event, the Li-2 served in the Czechoslovak air force and with ČSA, alongside the C-47s already delivered before the communist take-over.

Freedom flights

Such was the disdain that many Czechoslovak people held towards the Soviet-backed rule in their country from 1948 – during the Cold War – that there were numerous attempts made for escape to the West. A number

of these involved the successful hijacking or requisitioning of ČSA and air force Skytrains.

The trend began very soon after communist rule was established in Czechoslovakia. Many military veterans fled the country when the new communist government began to purge all those who had connections to the World War Two RAF. During June 1948, several air force personnel arrived at RAF Manston in Kent, having 'appropriated' one of the air force D-47 fleet.

A ČSA C-47A was hijacked during April 1948 to the airfield at Neubiberg, near Munich in West Germany. Up to 20 occupants are believed to have been involved.

The incident caught the authorities in both Czechoslovakia and West Germany by surprise.

However, far more spectacular were the events of March 1950, when three aircraft of ČSA were simultaneously hijacked. The trio subsequently landed at the USAF airfield at Erding, northeast of Munich. In total, from the three aircraft 26 of 85 occupants were recorded as wishing to stay in West Germany. The remaining extremely surprised passengers and crew returned to Czechoslovakia.

This was followed during March 1953 when ČSA C-47A 42-23523/OK-WDZ changed course from its scheduled route of Prague to the Czechoslovak city of Brno, and instead flew to Frankfurt in West Germany. It was deliberately re-routed there by its pilot who defected, together with five other people onboard, including the aircraft's navigator. The remaining occupants (Press reports at the time stated there were 29 persons on board in total) chose to return to Czechoslovakia.

Sadly, that aircraft was later to feature in one of ČSA's worst air disasters from the C-47 era. On January 18, 1956 it was destroyed in a Controlled Flight Into Terrain over eastern Czechoslovakia while en route from Bratislava on a scheduled flight. Of the 26 passengers and crew on board, just four survived.

Tragic events

It is a sad reality that a comparatively large number of the de-mobbed ex-USAAF and former US Navy C-47/R4D airframes that flooded the private and civil airline market following World War Two were involved in accidents. Many were non-fatal, but tragically some resulted in significant loss of life. For ČSA, the worst crash of a Skytrain was on December 21, 1948, when C-47A 43-93028/OK-WDN mysteriously flew into a hillside near Pilos, Greece, in bad weather… killing all 24 on board. It was on a flight with stopovers from Czechoslovakia to Israel. At that time Greece was embroiled in civil war, and claims arose at

the time that the aircraft had been accidentally shot down.

The Czechoslovak military was also not immune to tragic accidents. Several air force C-47s crashed, among them the unlucky 'D-13'. This airframe, former C-47B 43-49186, disintegrated at around 10,000ft in the region of Bánská Bystrica, Czechoslovakia, killing its crew and passengers, on July 3, 1956.

Retirement

Many surviving ČSA and air force airframes were gradually replaced and taken out of service during

the later 1950s and the start of the 1960s. Transport aircraft such as the Ilyushin Il-12 and Il-14/Avia 14 partly took over their short- and medium-haul roles.

Currently displayed at the Letecké Muzeum (Aviation Museum) at Kbely on the outskirts of Prague is a 1937-vintage DC-3-229, which has been painted to represent an air force D-47 coded 'D-21'. ●

Grateful thanks to my Czech colleagues and aviation contacts at the Military History Institute in Prague and the Letecké Muzeum at Kbely. Note: For ease of understanding, where applicable the translations of Czech names have been written capitalised in English.

LEFT Former C-47A 42-23602/OK-WDA was among the first Skytrains delivered to Czechoslovakia, and it received the ČSA number '01' (as seen on its fin). These aircraft were natural metal with blue trim, and bore the Czechoslovak flag on the rudder MALCOLM V LOWE COLLECTION

ABOVE The Letecké Muzeum's historic DC-3-229 was painted for many years to represent ČSA C-47A OK-XDM, and was displayed outside the ČSA company's former headquarters. Here it had just been returned to the museum, and is now painted as 'D-21' in military colours MALCOLM V LOWE

BELOW LEFT One of ČSA's demilitarised C-47 fleet, with a Junkers Ju 52/3m in the background. Passenger entry was on the port fuselage side between the wing and the tail, in keeping with the type's Skytrain origins MALCOLM V LOWE COLLECTION

Home
AND AWAY

Revel in these fascinating images of Dakota family airframes – based in the UK and overseas – courtesy of the **Graham Pitchfork** collection

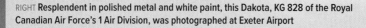

ABOVE **Testing low-speed sensing equipment and parachutes were just two of the roles of the Royal Aircraft Establishment's 'raspberry ripple' Dakota ZA947. The airframe is now operated by the RAF Coningsby, Lincolnshire-based Battle of Britain Memorial Flight**

RIGHT **Resplendent in polished metal and white paint, this Dakota, KG 828 of the Royal Canadian Air Force's 1 Air Division, was photographed at Exeter Airport**

ABOVE The aircraft of Air Viet Nam carried 'Hang Khong' wording on the fuselage, as demonstrated by this DC-3 (XV-NIB). The airline operated from 1951 until the end of the Vietnam war in 1975.

ABOVE Formerly the C-47B Dakota EI-ACH of Irish company Air Links, this airframe moved to the carrier Skyways of London, as G-APUC in 1959

BELOW Pictured here in the mid-1960s, this C-47, 0-76207, was a 'hack' aircraft for the USAF's 48th Tactical Fighter Wing at Lakenheath, Suffolk, UK, which flew F-100 Super Sabres at the time. It was eventually converted to an AC-47D gunship, but was shot down while over South Vietnam on May 4, 1968. Three crew members were killed, although four survived.

ABOVE **Normandie Air Services** flew regular services from Deauville and Rouen in France to Southampton, although the firm's **F-BEIG** shown here, an ex-USAF airframe, was photographed at Exeter

RIGHT **British United Island Airways**, which served routes across Europe but also between the Channel Islands and London Gatwick, was the owner of this smart C-47B **G-AMSV**

BELOW **Dakota TS423 'Mayfly'** flew with the Royal Aircraft establishment for a time, operating out of West Freugh, Dumfries and Galloway, Scotland as part of the Ferranti Flying Unit...which added the large radome visible here. For more details on this airframe see page 80

ABOVE **Shown parked at Exeter, Douglas C-47B G-ANAF of Top Flight operated Royal Mail flights from Newcastle, Tyne and Wear**

ABOVE **This C-47 registered N817NA, photographed at Edwards Air Force Base, California, flew with the USA's National Aeronautics and Space Administration**

SUBSCRIBE TODAY!

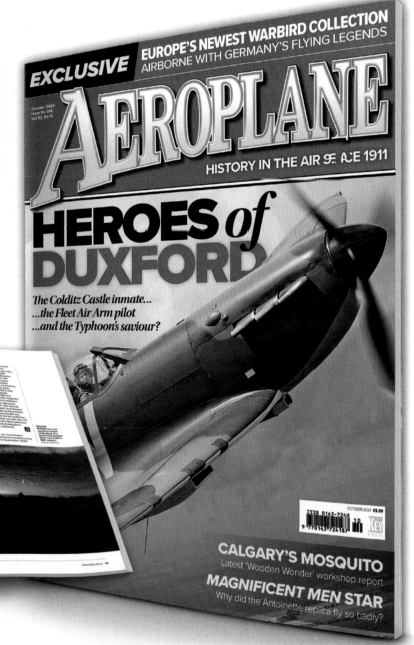

Aeroplane is still providing the best aviation coverage around, with focus on iconic military aircraft from the 1930s to the 1960s.

Blighty's 'DAKS'

FlyPast assistant editor **Jamie Ewan** provides an assessment of UK-based survivors of Douglas' indomitable DC-3/C-47 family

47 Air Dispatch Squadron, RAF Brize Norton, Oxfordshire – Dakota Mk.IV G-AMPO – marked as 'FZ625/YS-DH' – Gate guardian
Constructed as a C-47B-30-DK by Douglas at its Oklahoma City facility sometime in 1944, what is now G-AMPO was taken on charge by the USAAF as 44-76853, before joining the RAF as KN566 the following year. After its military service, the aircraft was registered G-AMPO and operated by the likes of Eagle Aircraft Services, Starways, Polaris Air Transport, Eastern Airways and Air Atlantique. Withdrawn from use, the aeroplane was donated to 47 Air Dispatch Squadron at RAF Lyneham, Wiltshire in 2001 and marked as 'FZ625/YS-DH', before following the unit to its current base at nearby Brize Norton in Oxfordshire.

Aces High, Dunsfold Aerodrome, Surrey – C-47A N147DC 'Mayfly' – marked as 42-100884 /A-S6 – Airworthy (also spends time at North Weald Airfield, Essex)
A stalwart of the European airshow circuit, N147DC is quite probably the world's lowest-timed flying Dakota, with fewer than 4,000 hours on the clock. Rolling out of Douglas' Long Beach factory in California, it joined the USAAF as 42-100884 on December 23, 1943. Allocated to the 79th Troop Carrier Squadron (TCS) at RAF Membury in Berkshire, it was in action over Normandy on D-Day the following year. Transferred to the RAF as TS423 in 1944, it later flew with the RCAF. Following the war, it served with Short Brothers, Scottish Aviation, Marshalls, Ferranti, and the Ministry of Technology, before being saved from the fire dump at Catterick, North Yorkshire, in 1979 by Aces High's Mike Woodley.

Aero Legends, Lydd Airport, Kent – C-47A N473DC – marked as 42-100882/P-3X *Drag 'em oot* – Airworthy (also spends time at North Weald Airfield, Essex)
Acquired by Aero Legends in 2017, *Drag 'em Oot* was built by Douglas at its Long Beach factory for the USAAF in early 1944. A veteran of both D-Day and Operation Market Garden, the aeroplane still sports more than 30 bullet holes from the latter following a skirmish with a Luftwaffe fighter. Christened for its role snatching gliders out of combat zones, it was later transferred to the RAF and assigned the serial TS422. Retired from military service in 1966 after serving with the RCAF, it made its way to the UK in 2005 (See *FlyPast* August 2019's *Return to Normandy*)

C-47B G-ANAF *Pegasus* – marked as KP220 – Airworthy (also spends time at North Weald Airfield in Essex)
See pages 84-90.

American Air Museum, IWM Duxford, Cambridgeshire – C-47A-85-DL G-BHUB – marked as 43-15509/S-W7 – Museum exhibit
Delivered to the USAAF on April 4, 1944, 43-15509 was assigned to the Ninth Air Force the following month. It was placed up for disposal in October 1945, after which the aircraft was employed by several carriers – including Scandanavian Airlines System as SE-BBH 'Vraken'. Returning to the US in 1951, it was registered N9985F and later N51V. It was then sold to the Spanish Air Force in 1962 and assigned the serial T.3-29, whereby it served with both Escuadrone 911 and 901 before being withdrawn on January 26, 1977. Acquired by

Aces High – then based at Duxford, Cambridgeshire – in 1980, it was then obtained by the Imperial War Museum, where it is currently suspended from the roof of the American Air Museum wearing its original wartime 37 TCS colours.

Battle of Britain Memorial Flight, RAF Coningsby, Lincolnshire – Dakota Mk.III ZA947 – marked as FZ692 *Kwicherbichen'* – Airworthy
Originally built as a C-47A by Douglas at Long Beach during 1942 and assigned the serial 42-24338, the aeroplane that became ZA947 was delivered to the USAAF on September 7, 1942, before being transferred to the RCAF under the Lend-Lease agreement around a week later. Re-designated as a Dakota Mk.III, it was allocated the RCAF serial '661' and served with that air arm until 1969 when it was declared surplus to requirements. It was then taken on charge by the UK's Royal Aircraft Establishment as KG661 in April 1969, being allocated the serial ZA947 in July 1979. Operated in a variety of roles until 1992, it was adopted by RAF Strike Command and sent to the BBMF in March 1993.

Night Fright C-47 Restoration Project, Coventry Airport, Warwickshire – C-47A-65-DL N308SF – Undergoing restoration (Access strictly by prior permission only)
Quite possibly one of the UK's most anticipated return-to-flight projects, what is now N308SF was taken on charge by the USAAF on November 2, 1943 as 42-100521, having rolled out of Douglas' Long Beach facility the previous month. Assigned to the 79th TCS, the aeroplane – christened

Night Fright – took part in every airborne mission across Europe during World War Two dropping paratroopers, towing gliders, evacuating wounded, and flying much needed supplies to the front line. Following the war, it passed through several private owners, and even served with France's Marine Nationale, before ending its flying days as a freighter in the US. For more on the Night Fright C-47 Restoration Project's efforts to return this legend to the skies, see *A Night To Remember, FlyPast* June 2020.

RVL Aviation, Coventry Airport, Warwickshire – Dakota Mk.IV G-AMPY – marked as KK116 – Airworthy

Having left Douglas' Oklahoma City production line as a C-47B-15-DK sometime in 1943 with the serial 43-49308, this airframe was first delivered to the USAAF,

before accepted by the RAF as KK116 in November 1944. Noted with Starways Ltd as G-AMPY on December 13, 1957, it served with various carriers including Air Jordan, Icelandair and Jersey European, before joining Air Atlantique at Jersey Airport on February 15, 1982. Remaining on its books until March 2000, it was listed with RVL Aviation until 2007, when it re-joined Air Atlantique's roster as part of the form's Classic Air Force (CAF). As it stands, G-AMPY is again registered with RVL and wears RAF Transport Command colours.

Skysport Engineering, Hatch, Bedfordshire – C-47A-85-DL N5595T – Stored (Access strictly by prior permission only)

Taken on charge with the USAAF as 43-15536 in mid-1944, this airframe was assigned to Air Transport Command on June 4

that year – however, little is known about its service during World War Two. Following the end of hostilities, it passed through several owners (including Piedmont Aviation) before being sold the Spanish Air Force on October 20, 1961 as T.3-27. Serving with Escuadrone 901 and 745, coded 901-7 and 745-27 respectively, it was withdrawn from use in February 1978. Registered G-BGCG later that year, it was subsequently flown to the UK, where it was purchased by US carrier Westair International as N5595T – but was never delivered. After being obtained by Skysport Engineering, N5595T has been stored since 1991.

Yorkshire Air Museum, Elvington – Dakota Mk.IV G-AMYJ – marked as 'KC427' – Ground runner

Manufactured by Douglas in its Oklahoma City factory as a C-47B-25-DK carrying the serial 44-76384, the Yorkshire Air Museum's example entered RAF service as KN353 in February 1945. In February 1953, it was purchased by Transair, registered G-AMYJ, and often assigned to troop-carrying charters. Operated by several carriers – including a spell in Egypt with Nile Delta Services as SU-AZF – it was bought by Air Atlantique at Coventry for pollution control work during the early 1980s. Withdrawn from use by the late 1990s and used extensively for spares, the aircraft was donated to the museum in December 2001, where it was restored to ground-running condition.

LEFT **Undergoing a comprehensive restoration to flight with Ben Cox's Coventry-based Heritage Air Services, 'Night Fright' is owned by Charlie Walker** KEY-JAMIE EWAN

BELOW **Douglas Dakota Mk.IV G-AMPY is currently maintained in airworthy condition by its registered owner – RVL Aviation.** KEY-JAMIE EWAN

RIGHT The South Yorkshire Aircraft Museum's Douglas DC-3 – N4565L – will be restored into the colours of BOAC's G-AGBB RICHARD E FLAGG

16 Air Assault Brigade HQ, Merville Barracks, Colchester – C-47B KP208 – marked as 'KG374/YS-DM' – Gate guardian

Built by Douglas as a C-47B-35-DK in Oklahoma City, 44-77087 was taken on strength by the USAAF in mid-1944, before being redesignated as a C-48-DO with the RAF later that year. Assigned the serial KP208, it became one of the last Dakotas in British service – having flown with the likes of the Coastal Command Communications Flight at Bovingdon, 24 Squadron, and the British Air Attache in India. After being retired in May 1970, KP208 was presented to the British Army's Parachute Regiment at Browning Barracks, Aldershot, Hampshire, where it was maintained by the Museum of the Airborne Forces. With the 'Paras' moving to Merville Barracks in 2009, KP208 was transported by road, refurbished, and finished in its current markings to represent 214 Squadron's 'KG374/YS-DM' – the machine Flt Lt David Lord was piloting when he earned a (posthumous) Victoria Cross in September 1944.

Metheringham Airfield Visitor Centre, Metheringham, Lincolnshire – Dakota Mk.III G-AMHJ – marked as KG651 – Undergoing restoration

Constructed as a C-47A-25-DK in Oklahoma during early 1944 for the USAAF, 42-108962 was diverted to the RAF as KG651 under the Lend-Lease programme that June. It was delivered to 109 Operational Training Unit, but also served with 24 Squadron, and 1333 Transport Support Conversion Unit before being withdrawn in October 1946. Like many post-war survivors of the type, KG651 had a successful civilian career flying with the likes of Pan African Air Charters, Cyprus Airways, British United Airways, Macedonian Airways and the Iraq Petroleum Transport Company, before joining Atlantic Air Transport at Coventry in 1987. The airframe continued to fly into the early 2000s, and was presented to the Assault Glider Trust at RAF Shawbury, Shropshire in November 2002, before being donated to the RAF Transport Command memorial North Weald. It arrived at Metheringham in late 2015 where it is currently undergoing restoration.

National Collections Centre/Science Museum Group, Wroughton, Wiltshire – DC-3A-197 EI-AYO – Stored (Access strictly by prior permission only)

One of the world's oldest surviving examples of the type, EI-AYO was originally delivered to United Airlines in New York on December 5, 1936 as NC16071. Serving solely with the carrier until 1954, the aeroplane later passed through several owners (including the Enhart Manufacturing Company) as N333H, N8695E, N255JB and N65556. Acquired by Skyways Inc as N655GP in 1969, it was flown across the Atlantic to continue plying its trade across Europe during the early 1970s with various airlines. Based primarily in Ireland, the machine was purchased by Commander Aircraft Sales and registered EI-AYO in February 1976, before being obtained by the Science Museum in late 1978. The aeroplane has remained with the organisation ever since – albeit in storage at Wroughton.

RAF Museum Cosford, Shropshire – Dakota C.4 KN645 – Museum exhibit

This machine was accepted on charge by the RAF under Lend-Lease on May 18, 1945, originally built by Douglas at Oklahoma City as a C-47-B-35-DK with the USAAF serial 44-77003. Joining a plethora of units – including the 2nd Tactical Air Force Communications Squadron, the Supreme Headquarters Allied Powers in Europe Communications Flight, the Queen's Flight and Malta Communications Flight, KN645 flew the type's last operational sortie in RAF service on April 1, 1970. Deemed a non-effective airframe, the aircraft was allocated to the RAF Museum on January 10, 1972. Originally moved by road to RAF Colerne in Wiltshire and allocated the ground instructional serial 8355M, KN645 arrived at RAF Cosford on October 16, 1975, where it remains today.

Dakota Mk.III N9050T (cockpit only) – Undergoing minor restoration – Michael Beetham Conservation Centre

Built as USAAF Skytrain 42-92648, in early 1944, this airframe was delivered to the RAF on February 14 that year. Redesignated as a Dakota III, the airframe was assigned the serial KG437. After delivery to 233 Squadron, the aeroplane took part in Operation Market Garden, before being sold to BOAC in 1946 as G-AGYX. Operated by BEA, Autair and United Libyan Airlines, it finally ended up in Sudan as 5N-ATA – however, by 1984 it was noted as being stored in Malta. Purchased by a private owner in 1991, the airframe was dismantled, before eventually being passed to the RAF Museum. With the nose restored by the Medway Aircraft Preservation Society, it was displayed at Hendon from January 2006, before being delivered to Cosford in early 2019.

Ridgeway Military and Research Group, Welford Park, Berkshire – C-47A-25-DK 42-93510 (cockpit only) – Museum exhibit (Visits only by prior arrangement)
Rolling out of Douglas' Oklahoma City factory, 42-93510 was accepted by the USAAF on May 27, 1944. Assigned to the Ninth Air Force the following month, the aircraft was soon in action supporting the Allied advance across Europe. Disposed of in 1946, the aeroplane was sold to Czechoslovakia's State Airline and registered OK-WAR, before being purchased by the French Air Force in May 1960. Serving with the likes of Groupe de Transport et de Liaison Aerienne (Air Transport and Liaison Group) 2/60 and Escadron de liaison aérienne (Air Liaison Squadron) 44, the aircraft was sold to Senegal as 6W-SAE on March 16, 1970. It was noted at a technical training centre at Dakar's Yoff Airport in 1979. Just the cockpit survives today.

Science Museum, Kensington, London – Dakota Mk.IV '448' (cockpit only) – Museum exhibit
Built in 1944 at Douglas' Oklahoma City factory in March 1945, C-47B-30-DK 44-76586 was taken on charge by the RAF as a Dakota Mk.IV with the serial KN448. Serving briefly with 10 Squadron, it joined 436 Squadron – part of the RAF/USAF/RCAF joint transport entity known as the 'Combat Cargo Task Force' – in October 1945 before being reassigned to 435 Squadron on March 17 the following year. Transferred to the RCAF on April 8, 1946 KN448 was withdrawn from service in 1968. With the aircraft scrapped the following year, only the cockpit survives – the Science Museum obtaining it soon after. It is currently on display within the attraction's 'Flight' Hall.

South Yorkshire Aircraft Museum, Doncaster, South Yorkshire – D-C3-201A N4565L – Undergoing restoration
Arriving at the South Yorkshire Aircraft Museum on August 6, 2003, N4565L originally rolled off Douglas' production line in Santa Monica during February 1939. Delivered to Eastern Air Line, it was allocated the fleet number '346' before being sold on several years later. Having changed hands privately several times, by 1961 it was registered as LV-GVP with the Ford Motor Company in Argentina, plying its trade as an executive transport. Fitted with a plush interior (including sleeping berths and a cocktail bar) it was said to be the most extravagantly equipped example of the type at that time. Currently undergoing a ground-up restoration, N4565L will be finished in the colours of DC-3 G-AGBB – the machine in which actor Leslie Howard lost his life on June 1, 1943 (see *Howard's End*, *FlyPast* February 2019)

Romney Marsh Wartime Collection, incorporating the Brenzett Aeronautical Museum Trust, Romney Marsh, Kent – Dakota IV G-AMSM (cockpit only) – Museum exhibit
Constructed as a C-47B-20-DK by Douglas at its Oklahoma City plant in 1943, this aircraft was originally accepted by the USAAF as 43-49948, before being transferred to the RAF and redesignated as a Dakota Mk.IV. Assigned the serial KN274, the aircraft served with the likes of 77 Squadron, Transport Command's Major Servicing Unit, and the station flight at St Eval in Cornwall, before its disposal in April 1952. Sold via the civilian market as G-AMSM soon after, the aircraft served with Starways and Kuwait National Airway, before joining cargo carrier Skyways in 1970. The aeroplane was written-off on August 17, 1978 while taking off from Kent's Lydd International Airport – the nose subsequently being acquired by the Brenzett Aeronautical Museum Trust.

Wings World War Two Remembrance Museum, Balcombe, West Sussex – C-47A -65-DL – marked as '2100766/4U/D *Lilly Bell II*' – Museum exhibit
Comprising the cockpit of former Senegalese AF C-47A 6W-SAF and the fuselage of ex-RAF C-47B FL586, this example of the Skytrain is a true hybrid. With 6W-SAF starting life as a 1942 Long Beach-built C-47A-65-DL, serialled 42-100611, FL586 rolled out of Oklahoma City around the same time as C-47A-1-DK as 42-92218. Assigned to the Ninth Air Force's 89th TCS, the original *Lilly Bell II* was lost with its crew near Jacobs Well, Guildford on October 25, 1944 – a dramatic shift in the aeroplane's centre of gravity caused by loose cargo resulted in 2100766 entering an inverted dive. ●

Honouring
A LEGEND...

"**I**t's one of the most iconic, versatile and beautiful aircraft ever designed!" enthuses Aero Legends founder Keith Perkins, as we discuss all things Dakota over a coffee in his hangar at Kent's London Ashford Airport. Close by sits both of his examples of Douglas' indomitable twin – the one and only *Drag 'em Oot*, a veteran of both D-Day and Operation Market Garden, and his latest addition, KP220 *Pegasus*, a former RAF machine built in 1945. Glancing over his shoulder towards the aeroplanes, the type's unmistakable lines being picked out by a nearby light, he reveals: "I fell in love with the Dakota after my first flight in one about ten years ago – that set me on the path to buying one." Following his gaze, I mention that age-old concern about the 'bottomless pit' of expenses and admin needed when it comes to owning and operating historic aircraft. He laughs: "It's not for the faint-hearted... or for those who haven't done their homework. These are *big* aircraft with even *bigger* running costs, so it made sense to operate them commercially. That way it helps cover the costs, and in return keeps them flying."

Highs and Lows
After forming the company in 2014, Keith has nurtured Aero Legends into what is the now the largest

As the UK prepared for its second national lockdown due to the ongoing COVID-19 pandemic, **Jamie Ewan** caught up with Aero Legends' Keith Perkins to find out about his new C-47, and his desire to form an 'airline' using Douglas' seemingly unsurpassable propliner

vintage aviation flight experience provider in the UK, with a star-studded fleet of Spitfires, Harvards and Tiger Moths – as well as *Drag 'em Oot* and *Pegasus*, the latter joining its roster in early June last year. While explaining how Aero Legends came about (see *Smooth Operator* in *FlyPast*, December 2018 for the full story) the conversation held in 2020 turned to that one word still dominating the world then – COVID. Keith

continued regarding the challenges Aero Legends faced at the time: "I'm stating the obvious when I say that it has impacted every area of our business – but what business hasn't it affected? That said, when I look back on this year there are some positives to take away – none more so than our customers remaining loyal and patient while we rearranged their flights. On a similar note, new bookings have continued at a steady pace for dates in 2021. As it stands, we are really looking forward to a very busy season next year. "Although we were

able to continue our Tiger Moth, Spitfire and Harvard experiences for a time, our Dakota operations came to a grinding halt. During a 'normal' year, both *Drag 'em Oot* and *Pegasus* will each fly about 100 hours, split across the likes of training and positioning flights, airshow appearances and our planned commemorative parachute drops over Normandy in June and Arnhem in September [see *Back to Normandy* in *FlyPast*, August 2019]. This year though, with almost every event cancelled, they were nowhere near that." Aero Legends resumed flight operations on April 12, 2021, and continues to offer

ABOVE **Prior to becoming 'Pegasus', G-ANAF – pictured here at Coventry on September 26, 2010 – gained this distinctive red and black scheme, which reportedly earned her the nickname 'Zorro'. Fitted with a bulbous radome, the aircraft was operated by Racal – later Thales – on radar development work connected with the Nimrod MR.4 programme** RICHARD E FLAGG

ABOVE **Seen here being escorted by Aero Legends Spitfire T.IX NH341 'Elizabeth' (closest) and Mk.IX TD314, Douglas C-47A Skytrain 42-100882 'Drag 'em Oot' joined the fleet in September 2017** AERO LEGENDS

RIGHT **'Drag 'em Oot' approaches Normandy on June 5, 2019 – the landing beaches visible in the distance – in preparation for the French-led 'D-Day 75' events** DARREN HARBAR

thrilling flight experiences to enthusiasts. Despite the UK's display season being decimated by COVID in 2020, both Daks were on duty for Aero Legends' own Battle of Britain Airshow held across September 25-27 at its Headcorn base in Kent (see *Remembering 'The Few'* in *FlyPast*, December 2020). Keith commented: "That was a huge highlight for us – they were definitely stars of the show. Not only was it the first time both Daks had flown together since the D-Day 75 commemorations in 2019, but it was also our first chance to properly show off *Pegasus* in public since it joined the fleet."

Saved from scrap

Built by Douglas at its Oklahoma City factory as a C-47B-35-DK, the aeroplane that is now *Pegasus* was originally accepted by the USAAF on June 8, 1945, before being quickly transferred to the RAF under the Lend-Lease agreement as Dakota Mk.IV KP220. Delivered to the UK via Canada soon after, it was assigned to 435 Squadron RCAF and used to support Canadian Army units stationed across Europe.

On March 6, 1946, KP220 was chosen as the personal mount of Air Officer Commanding 46 Group

(part of RAF Transport Command), AVM Arthur Leonard Fiddament, before joining 24 Squadron at Bassingbourn, Cambridgeshire a year or so later. After being used as a VIP transport, the aircraft was withdrawn from service in 1950 and delivered to 22 Maintenance Unit at Cumbria's RAF Silloth, where it was demilitarised and slated for disposal. Keith commented: "It looked like KP220 was destined to join the rest of its counterparts on Silloth's ever-growing pile of scrap metal. But in 1953 she was purchased by Southend, Essex-based BKS Aerocharter and registered G-ANAF – it was the start of a long

and successful career in civilian hands."

Operated by the likes of Hunting Aero Surveys in November 1958, followed by Westcountry Aircraft Servicing at Exeter in March 1977, the aircraft joined Air Atlantique (then based at Jersey on the Channel Islands) in October that year. Continuing, Keith noted: "Apart from a brief period when it was leased to British Caledonian in the late 1970s, G-ANAF was mainly used for ad hoc charter work before eventually finding its niche operating mail flights for the Post Office – something it continued to do until it and the contract

LEFT With remembrance and commemoration one of the biggest driving forces behind Aero Legends, both C-47s are at the forefront of its efforts. Here, 'Drag em Oot' releases 750,000 poppies over the White Cliffs of Dover in tribute to the fallen during 2019's Remembrance Sunday AERO LEGENDS

BELOW LEFT As a veteran of both D-Day and Operation Market Garden, 'Drag 'em Oot' is particularly sought after as a jump ship for commemorative and demonstration parachute drops. During 2019's D-Day 75 events in Normandy, it and 'Pegasus' dropped more than 1,000 parachutists
DARREN HARBAR

"These are big aircraft with even bigger running costs"

were transferred to Air Luton in June 1985."

Although the aircraft was reportedly operated by Topflight Aviation (see image on page 77) for a brief period, it was never registered to that operator. Having shown interest in purchasing G-ANAF in 1987, Miami-based charter service Starflite got as far as transferring it to the American N-Reg as N170GP, before the sale fell through. With the aircraft consequently staying in the UK, it was quickly returned to the British civil register.

After many years successfully plying its trade as a freighter, G-ANAF was selected to become a dedicated radar trials platform during the late 1990s. Fitted with a large and bulbous radome under her 'chin' and associated test equipment in the cabin, along with a multitude of fuselage aerials, the aircraft was regularly operated by aerospace and defence giant Racal Electronics, and later Thales.

Keith took up the story: "She was later painted in a bright red and black scheme and in 2015 was registered to the RVL Group, which converted her for marine surveillance and pollution dispersant spraying work on behalf of the Maritime & Coastguard Agency." Despite remaining on RVL's books and being maintained in airworthy condition, G-ANAF spent several years on the ground

>>>>>

ABOVE **Having been converted numerous times while in civilian hands, KP220 was returned as close to a stock C-47 as possible by Ben Cox and his team at Heritage Air Services – as revealed in this view looking towards the cockpit**
RICHARD FOORD AVIATION PHOTOGRAPHY

ABOVE RIGHT **With 'her' Twin Wasp engines growling away, Ben Cox and Jon Corley introduce 'Pegasus' to Headcorn for the first time on June 9, 2019 – shortly after the aeroplane joined Aero Legends' fleet**
RICHARD FOORD AVIATION PHOTOGRAPHY

ABOVE RIGHT **Aero Legends' C-47 'Pegasus' (left) in good company over Headcorn on September 26, 2020... 67 years after it was saved from the scrapman's axe**

at Coventry, before being sold to the airfield's Heritage Air Services in March 2019 and subsequently to Aero Legends. "Ben Cox and his team at Heritage Air Services did a fantastic job converting KP220 back to a 'stock' C-47. I decided to have *Pegasus* finished in RAF colours to complement *Drag 'em Oot* in its USAAF scheme," commented Keith.

With the work completed in time for the 75th anniversary of D-Day, the aircraft undertook its first post-restoration flight in the hands of Ben Cox and Jon Corley on June 5, before being flown to Cherbourg in France the following day to join *Drag 'em Oot* dropping parachutists. "*Pegasus* was the only example of the type to cross the [English] Channel on the actual anniversary of D-Day," commented Keith, before adding: "I think fate played a hand in us ending up with KP220 – when I saw that my initials made up part of its military serial, I had to buy it. A similar thing happened with *Drag 'em Oot*. When we were looking into its history, we found out that one of her pilots was Bruce Whiteford – an instructor with 435 Squadron when she served in post-war Canada. Unbelievably, he had also flown what is now the

flagship of our fleet, Spitfire T.IX NH341 *Elizabeth*, more than any other pilot during World War Two!"

While showing me around the aeroplane, Keith explained that remembrance and commemoration are the major driving forces behind Aero Legends: "We named KP220 *Pegasus* in recognition of the glider-borne assault on Pegasus Bridge during the opening minutes of the Allied invasion of Normandy, and in salute to the Pegasus Parachute Display Team, which we regularly work with."

One of the biggest challenges Aero Legends faces is recruiting experienced crews, particularly for its historic twins. "We want to bring younger pilots onto our roster. As such, until COVID, training was one of our biggest priorities. It's a dual issue – one is based around experience and type rating, and the other surrounds the difference between the US FAA's [Federal Aviation Administration] regulations and what we have here in the UK" explained Keith, before adding: "Aero Legends now has its own authorised training organisation, and with the long runway at our North Weald base, we will soon be able to instruct

DC-3 crews in-house – which is essential if we want these aeroplanes to continue flying.

"Most of those currently flying vintage aircraft are in their 50s and 60s, so we are looking to bring on the next generation of historic type-rated flyers. As well as encouraging new pilots, we want to be able to give the public the chance to fly in a military variant of the DC-3.

> ## "The long-lived Douglas twin is justifiably viewed as being among the greatest aircraft of all time"

However, it is all subject to getting the correct insurance – although many of the insurance companies have withdrawn their support from this side of the industry, which means getting the right cover isn't as straightforward as it once was. That said, the CAA has been very helpful in recognising the value of flying vintage aircraft, especially those of national importance."

Dakota legacy

The long-lived Douglas twin is justifiably viewed as being among the greatest aircraft of all time – and perhaps the finest ever. It popularised air travel and proved its profitability before excelling in times of conflict, serving for decades longer than its creators could possibly have envisaged.

Standing beside *Pegasus*, Keith mused: "It really is one of those types that just looks right, sounds right and *is* right. Even today, 85

years after it first flew, you can see the affection that the public has for it. Whenever *Drag 'em Oot* and *Pegasus* fly they get noticed, and our social media channels light up."

While chatting about the Dak's legacy, Keith pointed out that more than six decades after the last example of the type was delivered, DC-3s and C-47s (both modern iterations and those in their original configurations) are still plying their trade, carrying passengers and cargo around the world. "Aero Legends' mission is to make access to and flights in historic aircraft as accessible as possible, and the DC-3 is top of our list," he said. "The appetite from the UK public to fly in one is huge – to the extent that we receive countless requests from people to do just that. As such, I want to buy two more passenger-configured examples and use them to form an airline-type service from here at

Ashford, which has all the facilities we need.

"Our idea will be to initially operate 'A-to-B' trips around the UK with passengers able to buy single or multiple legs. While the Dakota is capable of carrying around 20 or so passengers, we will limit it to a maximum of ten to keep the experience special. The advantage with the Dak is you can stop off at places modern types can't, meaning we could offer customer flights to airshows and other events – similar to what Air Atlantique used to do."

However, due to the fact the DC-3 is operated on a Certificate of Airworthiness – or CoA – as opposed to a Permit to Fly, the Safety Standards and Consent (SSAC) route that Aero Legends uses for its Spitfire flight experiences isn't an option. "We will need to operate these DC-3

RIGHT **To close its Battle of Britain Airshow on all three days, Aero Legends flew a spectacular 'balbo' with its C-47s, Spitfires and Harvards. Now imagine it with four Dakotas!** KEY-JAMIE EWAN

BELOW **Built in 1945, 'Pegasus' is one of around 150-plus examples still earning a living. As Keith Perkins said: "It really is one of those types that just looks right, sounds right and is right."** RICHARD FOORD AVIATION PHOTOGRAPHY

passenger flights under an Air Operators Certificate [AOC] obtained from the Civil Aviation Authority [CAA]. By law, an AOC is needed by any individual, or organisation that wants to operate an aircraft for the purpose of commercial air transport. We were well on the way to setting up our own AOC, but plans have been delayed due to COVID," commented Keith.

Back to the battlefields
As well as UK routes, it is hoped Aero Legends can further expand its commemorative activities across Europe, as Keith alluded: "We will also offer regular flights to Normandy and Arnhem which I think will

be very popular, especially with American visitors. Now that the UK has left the EU, we will have to wait to see what we'll be allowed to do."

Similarly, the CAA will have to leave the EASA [European Union Aviation Safety Agency], meaning it will be responsible for fulfilling its own regulatory functions. Keith continued: "As you can imagine the financial commitment for this, especially with regard to training, spares, and engineering, is significant, but we are moving the plans forward. Our engineering team at Vintage Aero [part of Vintage Legends, the group that owns Aero Legends] are already busy familiarising themselves with our Dakotas, and the 1930s technology

around which they were designed and built."

As for acquiring a new DC-3, which will most likely be finished in a polished aluminium scheme in salute to the classic propliner's heyday, Keith explained: "I've already got my eye on several – however, the dilemma is that the best options aren't currently on the UK register, so I need to balance the attraction of taking on a superb aeroplane against the uncertainty that came with converting it to the British register. While there are others that already

> ## "I want to buy two more passenger-configured examples"

have a G-reg, they would need more investment to configure them correctly for what we want to do. It's definitely a game of swings and roundabouts!"

While thanking Keith for his time, one thought inevitably came to mind. The next time I visit Ashford, I'll most likely be stepping back in time aboard a DC-3, and I can't wait… ●

For more information about Aero Legends and the experiences on offer, visit: *www.aerolegends.co.uk* or call 01622 812 830

TRIUMPHANT
RETURN TO THE AIR

Mike Haskew investigates the story of one of the quickest Dakota restorations ever.

RIGHT **The left wing of CF-DTD sits ready for reattachment while work continues outdoors at Saint-Hubert** PIERRE GILLARD

It was nothing short of a miracle, some would say. However, all would agree that it was a triumph. The return of a venerable Dakota airframe to the skies was completed with a memorable flight on the 75th anniversary of D-Day on June 6, 2019, and the commitment of a dedicated group of air devotees, respectful of the tradition and heritage they were intent on preserving, made it possible.

Aviation enthusiast, collector and amateur historian Benoit de Mulder sees the restoration of a D-Day and Operation Market Garden airframe as one of the great events of his life. Sure, there were ups and downs, difficulties that led down the long road, but in the end the effort was a great success. In cooperation with Mikey McBryan of Buffalo Airways, a Canadian transport line based in Yellowknife, Northwest Territories, Hay River, and Edmonton, Alberta, and a host of volunteers and aviation experts, a piece of history was saved in grand style and in a stunningly short period of time.

The story began long ago, when the C-47A-5-DK Skytrain with factory serial number 12253

RIGHT **The cockpit of CF-DTD is shown during the extensive restoration that was required to make the DC-3 airworthy once again** BENOIT DE MULDER

was completed at the Midwest City Douglas Aircraft factory in Oklahoma City. One of more than 5,300 C-47s produced at the facility from March 1943 through the end of World War Two, the aircraft was completed sometime that year and then handed over to the British Royal Air Force in February 1944 through the Lend-Lease programme. Redesignated FZ668, the Dakota, as the British called the C-47, was assigned to No.271 Squadron RAF by the end of the month and went on to participate in the airlift of Allied paratroopers that opened the D-Day invasion

of Normandy to liberate Western Europe from Nazi occupation. In the autumn of 1944, FZ668 also took part in the ambitious airborne/ground offensive into the southern Netherlands dubbed Operation Market Garden. By the end of World War Two, the plane had also served in the China-Burma-India theatre.

A true relic of the great global conflict, the plane became surplus and was sold to Canadair and converted to passenger service with Trans-Canada Airlines as CF-TER, its first flight on April 4, 1947, and its last a decade later. From there, the subject aircraft was purchased by the Canadian Department of Transportation and redesignated CF-DTD, last flying with Transport Canada in the early 1990s. Donated to the Fondation Aerovision, whose intent was to open an aviation museum, the aircraft reached Saint-Hubert, Quebec, but the plans for the museum soon foundered. Sadly, the plane fell into disrepair, and vandals stole components, leaving damage to the plane, and relegating it to an almost forgotten status. A real link to the past had begun to deteriorate, virtually unnoticed.

Enter Benoit de Mulder. Almost on a whim, he bought the derelict plane from Aerovision with the idea of restoration. "I don't know what was going on in my head," he remembered, "but I said yes, and the price was right. The aircraft was going to be completely scrapped, and my goal in 2017 was to restore it myself as a static Trans-Canadian Airlines plane from the 1950s, to the TCA standard, and it was going to take five to seven years I thought."

Benoit inspected the aircraft and found it had deteriorated substantially, home to birds, rodents, and wasps, much of its original equipment and fixtures

stripped away by robbers. The tail wheel was mired deep in mud, and it took assistance from several friends and the help of the École nationale d'aerotéchnique (ENA), based in Saint-Hubert, to get the project going. Still, there were challenges. Financial support was difficult to come by, and Benoit invested personally of his own resources to keep the possibility of restoration alive. At length, he realised that more help was needed.

eBay D-Day

"Finally, I was looking for someone to buy it," he said, "for a way to get people interested. I put it on eBay with a $10,000 price, and soon I had everybody looking at it. Basler and others called with the possibility of doing a conversion. Then, I had a call from Mikey, and he had decided that he wanted the plane to fly again for the 75th anniversary of D-Day. He wanted to get the get the airplane in airworthy condition in less than six months."

McBryan, whose Buffalo Airways had achieved some degree of fame with the hit reality History Television show *Ice Pilots* that ran for six seasons from 2009-2014, had long admired the DC-3 and

stepped in to make the purchase. Even though his original plan for a renewal of the *Ice Pilots* series did not materialise, Mikey maintained a vision with his Plane Savers project. "I had this airplane and an idea," he explained. "I could not quit. I could not let this idea die. So, I did the only thing I could think of. I grabbed my GoPro and logged into my dormant YouTube account. The rest is history."

McBryan chronicled the Herculean effort that resulted in the restoration of CF-DTD in record time. True to their goal, the volunteers gathered on that sunny June 6, 2019, in Saint-Haubert to witness the fruit of their

long labour. CF-DTD's engines roared, and the plane took to the sky in triumph. A new chapter in the storied life of this historic aircraft had begun.

"We were working seven days a week from 6am to 10pm," recalled Benoit, who authored the book *DAKOTA #12253 A Plane Savers Story* to document the incredible restoration journey. "It was a group of volunteers from everywhere. The volunteers were fantastic, and some 40 people participated in the effort. The real work began in April." When the amazing effort was completed, Benoit concluded: "This flight is not only a massive technical achievement, in just three months returning to the sky an aircraft abandoned for almost 30 years. It is also the realisation of a dream supported by all who worked tirelessly to save this aircraft and to show that with goodwill, knowledge, and passion everything is possible."

According to Benoit, approximately 1,000 people attended the D-Day flight, and then CF-DTD was a popular attraction at the following Oshkosh air show. Today, the aircraft – in its restored glory – resides in Red Deer, Alberta, Canada. ●

ABOVE LEFT **In all its restored glory, CF-DTD flies again after a remarkable restoration project that gave the DC-3 airframe new life** BENOIT DE MULDER

ABOVE RIGHT **A forklift brings the starboard engine of DC-3 CF-DTD in position for placement within the aircraft** BENOIT DE MULDER

LEFT **Inside the hangar at Saint-Hubert work continues at a rapid pace to bring CF-DTD back to life** PIERRE GILLARD

LEFT **A crowd gathers in anticipation of the historic flight of CF-DTD to commemorate the 75th anniversary of D-Day and its own participation in that long ago historic event** PIERRE GILLARD

Latin
WORKHORSE

Santiago Rivas explores Colombia's La Vanguardia Airport, where Douglas' immortal DC-3 still provides a much-needed lifeline flying passengers and freight across rugged landscapes

Despite being 2024, the city of Villavicencio, the capital of Colombia's Meta Department, is home to an airport that still reverberates to the radial growl of classic propliners… La Vanguardia. Acting as the gateway to the South American country's remote eastern plains (known locally as 'the other half of Colombia') its population's density, along with its economic and urban development, are significantly lower than those in the nation's west. For this and other reasons, much of this vast tropical region is served by none other than Douglas' legendary DC-3.

Propliner revolution
The airport at Villavicencio traces its roots back to the days

of Sociedad Colombo Alemana de Transportes Aéreos (SCADTA), which translates as The Colombian-German Air Transport Company – the predecessor of the country's flag carrier Avianca. Having first

built an aerodrome at nearby Apiay, it was appropriated by the Colombian Air Force in 1933 and christened San José del Guaviare Air Base. As a result, SCADTA turned its attentions to another site

on the banks of the Guatiquía River, just north of Villavicencio.

Today, La Vanguardia boasts a 2,000m runway, radar control facilities, several hangars and infrastructure belonging to numerous airlines, a small terminal building for passengers and is dubbed the 'DC-3 capital of the world'.

During the early 1990s, Villavicencio became a dream for lovers of classic propliners when several Colombian carriers flying the likes of the DC-3, DC-4, DC-6, and C-46 from Bogotá's El Dorado International Airport were asked to leave. As such, many moved to Villavicencio to continue plying their trade across the Amazon. However, due to a combination of factors, progress at La Vanguardia has always been slow. And with

many towns across eastern Colombia suffering from a similar lack of development and few transport links, most are served solely by rudimentary landing strips – requiring an aeroplane capable of operating from such runways. Add to this the cost of flying long distances over the unforgiving Amazon rainforest and there are very few viable options. Yet, despite its design dating to 1935, the DC-3 is still the perfect machine for the job – to the point that, even into the 21st century, 'new' airframes continued to arrive. The age-old saying of: "the only replacement for a DC-3 is another DC-3" has never been truer.

Having flown these venerable machines from Villavicencio for almost three decades, the operators have formed their

own fraternity – everyone, be it pilots, mechanics, dispatchers or administrative personnel, knows each other. With several of the resident airframes having been owned by most of the various carriers, some have survived the birth and decline of the firms to which they belonged, while others have been returned to the skies instead of rusting away as wingless hulks. It would be easy to say that La Vanguardia holds an almost eternal atmosphere, accompanied by the smell and sound of the DC-3's faithful Pratt & Whitney Twin Wasp engines.

D-Day stripes and tragedy

Although Villavicencio is nowhere near its former propliner heyday, it still hosts several DC-3 operators, although as it stands just two are left flying the

ABOVE **An Air Colombia DC-3 undergoes maintenance outside the operator's facilities at Villavicencio. Founded in 1987, this carrier was one of those affected by the hike in insurance costs following the loss of HK-2494** ALL SANTIAGO RIVAS

BELOW **Polished lifeline: Aerolineas del Llano's last operational DC-3 (HK-3215) departs Villavicencio on a revenue flight. With few roads, and waterborne transport taking several days at a time, most of the Amazonian villages rely on these aeroplanes to stay connected**

>>>>

type – Aerolineas Andinas S.A. (ALIANSA) and Aerolineas del Llano S.A.S (ALLAS). That said, Air Colombia, which ceased trading in September 2019, continues to operationally maintain two of its three examples. Sadly, the situation for Colombia's DC-3-equipped carriers became incredibly complicated following the loss of Latinoamericana de Servicios Aereo's (Laser Aéreo) airframe HK-2494 on March 9 last year, during a non-scheduled passenger flight; all 14 on board were killed. Although it was possible to avoid completely banning the type's operation in the country, as some had suggested, the enormous increase in insurance costs made any use of the type almost unprofitable for most. As a result, while there was around a dozen or so operational DC-3s in 2014, just four remain today – one with ALLAS, while the others are in use with ALIANSA. Of the latter, HK-5016 is a DC-3-65TP equipped with Pratt & Whitney PT-6A-65 turbine engines, purchased from South Africa in 2014. As well as the previously mentioned Air Colombia airframes, other examples are stored in various states around the airport. Although, it can't be

said they have flown for the last time, as each could be returned to the skies thanks to Villavicencio's experienced engineers – without them, these 70-year-old machines wouldn't fly at all.

Located at the western end of the airport is ALIANSA. Formed on August 29, 1989, it has had a chequered past – punctuated by Colombia's ongoing internal conflict. With its operation interrupted for several years during the early 2000s, its fleet of DC-3s, acquired from the defunct carrier VIARCO (Vías Aéreas de Colombia), are adorned with D-Day invasion stripes.

While it may seem odd these world-renowned black and white markings are flying over the

> **"Formed during 1992, ALLAS is an example of the mechanical wizardry that occurs at Villavicencio"**

Colombian tropics well into the 21st century, it is all down to the arrival of HK-4700.

Constructed as a C-47A by Douglas at its Long Beach factory in California sometime during 1942,

this former USAAC and US Navy machine was exported to Colombia from the Netherlands in April 2010, having passed through numerous private owners around the world. Wearing facsimile RAF markings, invasion marks and *Fifi Kate* nose art when it arrived, everything but the stripes were removed – these then being adopted by most of its stablemates, apart from HK-5016. With one of the biggest offices and maintenance areas at the airport, ALIANSA also has a large warehouse and a dedicated engine test area.

Engineering wonders

Continuing east you come to Sociedad Aérea Del Caquetá or SADELCA which, although having ceased flying in 2014, has maintained plans to recommence its operation. One of the carriers that moved to Villavicencio from El Dorado, it flew a mixed fleet of Antonov An-30s and -32s alongside its DC-3s. At the time of its closure, SADELCA had four machines split between Villavicencio and San José del Guaviare (200 miles to the southeast) serving the region – including HK-2494, which was later sold to Láser Aéreo.

Another of SADELCA's DC-3s, HK-1149, arrived in the country during the 1960s from the US Federal Aviation Administration (FAA), and provided invaluable services as a radio calibrator with Colombia's own Civil Aviation Administration for almost 30 years. To this day, the aircraft still carries an extra observation window on each side.

After crossing most of the airport's apron there is another set of hangars – one being the home of ALLAS, which shared its facilities and staff with Aerovanguardia before it stopped operating in 2007. Formed during 1992, ALLAS is an example of the mechanical wizardry that occurs at Villavicencio. Its first airframe, HK-3215, was grounded for almost 15 years having been practically abandoned at the airport. However, after a period of restoration, which included acquiring new engines, the machine was returned to the skies. Working alongside its other example – N293WM, which arrived from the US in 2013 – only HK-3215 remains operational today.

The next company with DC-3s on its books is Air Colombia, which owns the best facilities at Villavicencio by far, although as previously mentioned, it suspended its operations in September 2019. Having operated the venerable DC-6 for many years, the four-engined propliner lost out to several other more economical types – in particular, the DC-3. As a result, its last surviving 'Six' (HK-1700) was scrapped during 2012.

ABOVE **Pictured in 2013, DC-3 HK-2494 taxies past one of its modern stablemates – Antonov An-32 HK-4296**

ABOVE RIGHT **Just another day under the Colombian sun for HK-2494 at La Vanguardia**

RIGHT **DC-3 capital of the world! With Air Colombia's HK-3293 holding for departure, another example is seen on final approach to La Vanguardia. Despite several carriers looking to replace their examples with more modern aircraft, the associated operating costs skyrocketed. As such, the venerable Douglas type has continued to 'outlive' them – until now**

BELOW **With the ground handlers heading to their next task, SADELCA's HK-2494 gets ready to taxi at Villavicencio under a vivid blue sky**

Among Air Colombia's pilot roster is Capt Joaquín Sanclemente – one of the country's most experienced DC-3 exponents with more than 10,000 hours. His love and passion for the type can be seen by the 'Dak' nose he has in his home, as well as his refusal to fly for a more 'modern' airline.

No end in sight

Next, there is Aerolineas Llaneras, or ARALL – a carrier that once operated a pair of DC-3s, together with its current fleet of Cessna types. Although its Douglas twins have not flown for several years, they are stored, albeit wingless, alongside several examples of de Havilland's rugged DHC-2 Beaver.

Finally, there is Laser Aéreo – located on La Vanguardia's most eastern apron – which owns a repair shop capable of keeping the DC-3s in the air. As well as its maintenance operation, Laser Aéreo regularly flew its own fleet of machines, including *Fifi Kate* and HK-2494 – the latter purchased from SADELCA following its closure. As well as being the so-called 'DC-3 capital of the world', La Vanguardia maintains several other classics, most of which have

already been retired – including several Antonov An-2s, as well as the only An-12 in Latin America. Despite the hardships and often uncertain times, the rugged Andean peaks will keep these much needed

and revered workhorses flying for several years to come. Combining today's regulations with historic aviation, it is curious to find modern safety cards on board Douglas' quite incredible DC-3… ●

BUILD HISTORY, PIECE BY PIECE

5743
SCALE: 1:48
DOUGLAS™ C-47
SKYTRAIN (DAKOTA)

896 🧱 2 👤

MADE OF HIGH QUALITY BRICKS

AVAILABLE FROM ALL GOOD HOBBY STORES

MADE IN EU
POLAND

www.cobibricks.com

Dakota Mk. III

№ 1338 model kit
modèle réduit

1:72 scala scale

® ITALERI

The "Dakota"

The twin-engine Douglas DC-3 was definitely one of the most famous transport aircraft of aviation history thanks to its reliability, flexibility and service life. During the Second World War it was developed a version dedicated to military duties: the Douglas C-47 Skytrain.
Produced in large numbers by American production plants, was used extensively by the Allies on all fronts. In particular, the C-47s received by British Royal Air Force and Commonwealth Air Forces took the name "Dakota" and they were used for logistic, tactical transports, launch of paratroopers and medical evacuation.
Thanks to its two Pratt & Whitney 1,200 HP engines the "Dakota" was able to reach a top speed of 360 Km/h. It had a pay-load of 2,500 Kg or a capacity of 28 troops.

RAF, Squadron 233
Blackhill Farm-Swindon, Wiltshire, U.K. 1944/45.

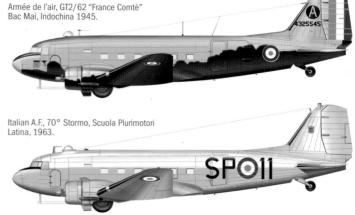

Armée de l'air, GT2/62 "France Comtè"
Bac Mai, Indochina 1945.

USAAC, 80th TCS, 436th TCG
Membury, Berkshire, U.K., 1945.

Italian A.F., 70° Stormo, Scuola Plurimotori
Latina, 1963.

Ask your local distributor or contact: Italeri S.p.A.- via Pradazzo, 6/b 40012 - Calderara di Reno - Bologna - Italy - www.italeri.com

A Churchyard Diary

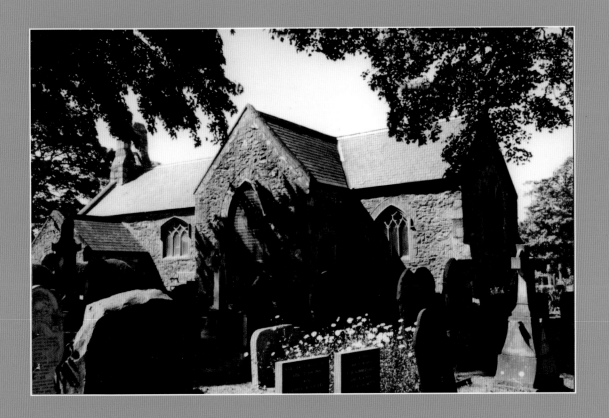

A record of the plants, flowers and trees in St. Hilary's
Churchyard, Llanrhos, during 1999.

Text and Drawings by Betty Mills.
Photographs by Maurice J Mills